A BOY FROM SURREY

IMPRESSIONS OF A LIFETIME

JOHN PRIEST

An early interest in planes and weather shaped the rest of John Priest's life, from becoming a meteorologist in the RAF to spending the best year of his life on a flying boat base in Sicily. His extensive knowledge of planes made him an excellent guide in latter years at Croydon Airport Museum.

Amazing memories! Crisp snapshots of life from the 1930s, through the Second World War years, to a varied career with the BBC from its early days, until retirement and worldwide travels.

Treasured photographs illustrate just a fraction of the author's fascinating life, making this an engaging and vivid memoir with flashes of humour throughout – precious details preserved for future generations.

© John Priest 2015

ISBN 978-1-78003-833-9

Published using the services of
www.easyBookpublishing.co.uk

Author Essentials
4 The Courtyard
South Street
Falmer BN1 9PQ

www.authoressentials.com
info@authoressentials.com

Cover design by Jacqueline Abromeit

ACKNOWLEDGMENTS

My very good friends Ding and his wife Moon have been the greatest help to me in typing my manuscripts on the computer together with the wide variety of photos.

My next door neighbours Robert and Jane Cleeve have also shown great kindness in helping me during awkward periods of hospital activities, and Jane completed the typing of the last three and a half chapters.

My long-standing friends, Melanie, Caroline and Felicity, the three daughters of Dr Ian Smith and his wife Mary, have also shown great interest in my efforts and made practical suggestions. Felicity in fact did the early stages of typing my manuscripts on the computer but had to hand over to Ding when her theatrical affairs became a priority.

Finally, I'd like to thank Jackie who runs the Corner Gallery at 11 Beeches Avenue (which was my grandfather's home) for suggesting the title of my book.

The Priest family in 1903,
showing my father sitting on his father's knee.

CONTENTS

CHAPTER 1

Early Days

I have lived in the same house for over 90 years, and in 2006 I was persuaded to become a guide at the Croydon Airport Museum, which is about 10 miles due south of London. It was not long before my colleagues noticed that I could talk about many occasions dating back to the mid 1920s without having to refer to any notes, and when we discussed this my explanation was that I had actually experienced most of the events that I described and could remember them in great detail. They then said I should write them down for the benefit of those who would follow. That is how the seed was sown for me to write about a lifetime of my impressions.

I decided to begin in 1924 when I was two, because at that time my parents moved to Carshalton from the council house at Bessels Green near Sevenoaks where I was born. This was their first home when they got married in 1921 and the new place must have created quite an impression on me which is why I have early memories as far back as this.

My mother came from a family of butchers and farmers in the nearby village of Chipstead. Her father had built up a thriving business of three shops in Kent and a farm in Devon. He had two sons and three daughters, but one of the daughters was burned to death when she was five – more about this later.

One of my earliest memories, coinciding with moving into the new home, is sitting in a high chair in the kitchen with a blue bib around my neck and my mother was feeding me with some hard boiled egg and melted butter in a teaspoon and she said, "Open your mouth, here comes a puffer train." Every detail is crystal clear, even the appearance of my mother who was then 33 years old. Also at about the same time I remember having my feet washed in the bathroom while sitting in the soap dish with my feet in the washbasin, but I can't remember anything else except that it was in the house where I have remained to this day and that blue bib is still in the sideboard drawer.

The great thing about talking with old friends is that a chance remark will often spark off a memory of something interesting which until that moment you thought you'd forgotten about it. That's how these two early stories came back after so many years buried in the subconscious.

The main reason for moving from Bessels Green was because the house we moved to in Carshalton was owned by my father's family who were house builders. My paternal grandfather was a very successful speculative builder before and after the First World War. He built many houses in Wallington and Carshalton where he lived in Beeches Avenue until he died in 1925. My father was the youngest of seven brothers, and he and his elder brother Albert were very close as there was only one year between them. From about 1907, they both sang in the choir at Carshalton Parish Church, almost until they and the other brothers joined the army on the outbreak of war in 1914 and miraculously they all returned safely to civilian life in 1920 in spite of many perilous episodes throughout these war years. When Albert got a girlfriend, she was the daughter of Mr Woodman, the butcher in Carshalton High Street and the name can still be seen on the front of what was his shop next to the parish church facing the pond. As Mr Woodman visited Smithfield Market on a regular basis, he got to know another butcher, Mr Wisdom (my mother's father) from Sevenoaks who had two daughters. Albert heard about this and suggested to his brother Frank (my father) that they should cycle to Sevenoaks so that my father could meet the two daughters. The result was that one of them Annie (known as Ann for the rest of her life) became my mother when Frank married her in 1921. I did have a sister when I was eight, but she only lived for three months. In those days, when my mother went to the nursing home to have the baby, I thought people went to those places to choose a baby where they were all lined up sitting on shelves.

As my mother came from a farming community I can remember from a very early age visiting the lovely old farmhouse dating back to the early seventeenth century. Even in the 1930s they still lit the kitchen with its huge central table with a gas lamp which made a gentle 'plop' when it was lit. Very often a corner of the kitchen would have a small piglet wrapped in a blanket huddled up in one of the cats' baskets. This was probably the weakest of a new litter of pigs which lived in a sty by the river at the bottom of the garden.

I've still got a snapshot of me aged about 4 or 5 with a watering can going to put water in a bowl just outside a chicken coop where the hen was fussing about over a lot of little fluffy yellow chicks.

This sort of life dominated my school years because I always spent a large part of my school holidays staying with my grandfather and his two sons, Jim and Char, and daughter Edie, none of whom ever got married, and generally taking part in the day-to-day activities. I even used to help, where I could, in the slaughter house and was quite immune to the gory sights that went on there. That is until about 15 years later when I went through a phase of the most horrible nightmares. I don't think my uncles ever really got over the disturbing jobs they had to do because I can remember hearing one of them say as he got hold of a sheep, "Come here you poor little bugger."

Although my mother had two sisters and two brothers she was the only one who got married and when she was nine, her younger sister who was then five died in a tragic accident when she caught her nightdress alight carrying a candle to go to bed. This event became a true ghostly experience for me many years later in 1988, but that story will come later.

When my parents, Ann and Frank, got married on 27th June 1921 (which was the same date my mother died in 1992 when she was one hundred), they lived in a council house very near my mother's old home. There was a branch railway line station quite nearby called Chevening Halt and my father travelled from here to London every day to the Stock Exchange where he started work at the end of the First World War. His father was a speculative builder in Dulwich but he was doing so well at the turn of the century that he decided to move to Carshalton around 1906 to take advantage of the rapid expansion of suburban housing.

One day my father came home from London and said to my mother, "Ma says that if we'd like to move to Carshalton they will let us live in one of the Priest Houses rent free." My mother replied, "I'm not going to live up there," to which my father said, "Well you can bloody well stay here, because I'm going."

They moved in 1924. Because I was an only child my mother was over-protective and I hadn't even started school when I was 5. This prompted a Schools Inspector to call one day and ask which school I was attending to which my mother replied, "Oh we have a private tutor for him." This amazingly was accepted without any further questions and the inspector left.

My parents' Wedding Day, 27th June 1921.

Their first home at Bessels Green.

My mother's family home and butcher's shop at Chipstead Kent.

Old Rose (the horse) in retirement, after years of delivering meat.

Helping out on the farm with my watering can.

CHAPTER 2
School

It wasn't long after this that I started at St Hilda's, the nearby kindergarten. That first day stands out vividly, especially the entrance hall with the smell of its polished floorboards and shoe bags on hooks all round the walls where you took off your outdoor shoes and put them in the orange bags after putting on plimsoles.

My first lesson was tracing round the pieces of cardboard cut into shapes for the letters of the alphabet and I can remember tracing round the outline of a snake which was in the shape of a letter S. Miss Moore was the teacher and she wore long plaits of hair in the shape of flattened buns over each ear. Strange to say I have no memory at all of coming home after that first day at school.

Soon after starting at St Hilda's we used to pass a house where a little girl called Rosemary was also getting ready to go to the same school. Rosemary's mother was always in a terrible muddle, so it seemed quite natural for us to knock on the door each day and for Rosemary to come with us. This led to a lifelong friendship between our two families.

Rosemary's father, Mr Newbald, was a dentist. He came from the Isle of Wight and in later years I loved staying at their family home in a little side street about 200 yards from Ryde seafront. Their house had the most marvellous atmosphere of serene peace and quiet with Victorian cut-glass chandeliers, heavy curtains and a very large kitchen and pantry. Mrs Rose was Mr Newbald's sister and she had that same air of calm about her as her house. I don't know what happened to her husband but it seems very likely she lost him during the First World War because when it was over, she applied for the post of Personal Assistant to Dame Nellie Melba and got it. This led to worldwide travels with the singer until

Melba retired. I was staying with Rosemary in Ryde when we were about seven or eight, and another sister, Ella Newbald also lived with Mrs Rose. Poor Ella was so different, never married, tall, thin, gaunt, very shy and timid and when she smiled she looked as though she was about to burst into tears. One incident with Ella I remember very clearly. Rosemary and I were going to have our breakfast on the lawn in front of the house one hot summer's day, and Ella offered to bring our cornflakes out to us. There was plenty of milk and sugar already on the cornflakes when they arrived. We took one mouthful and had to spit it all out again immediately. Ella had mistakenly sprinkled salt instead of castor sugar. When she saw what we did, she said, "Oh I didn't think it would make any difference!"

About this time, 1928 or so, my father bought a Morris Cowley, a four-seater open tourer. When you put the hood up, the separate windows made of mica slotted into holes in the tops of the doors and bodywork. He paid just under £13 a month for a year for it, which in today's money would come to something like £16,000, so cars were not cheap in those days. My mother was a very nervous passenger even though the roads were nearly empty, so I usually sat in the back with her. Once when we were on our way to Sevenoaks to my mother's family home, she asked my father to go a bit slower but he didn't take any notice, so she shouted at him and took off one of her shoes and hit him on the back of the head with the heel. It's a good job they weren't stiletto heels. On another occasion, our route from Carshalton to Sevenoaks took us past Croydon Airport. In those days before the new airport opened in 1928, the main road went right through the middle of the airfield with level crossing gates, just like the railways, to hold up the traffic while an airliner crossed the road from the hangars to the passenger terminal. We were held up as the big three-engined bi-plane (probably an A W Argosy) went across the road under its own power. The pilot was sitting in the open cockpit wearing a trilby hat, which he politely raised to us for waiting for him. Since these very early days I have become intensely interested in Meteorology and Civil Aviation and for the past six years or so have been a guide at the Croydon Airport Museum which is housed in the original Control Tower and Terminal Booking Hall building.

I'm one of the few people who have actual memories of the old airport which, as already mentioned, came to an end when the new airport opened in 1928 beside the recently built Purley Way. Fortunately my memory is good enough to recall many events right up to the final closure of the airport in September 1959.

Reverting to my very early school days, my parents and I spent many happy holidays with both sets of grandparents: one of them in farm-like surroundings, the other, on my father's side, in a family hotel on the seafront at Worthing where Grandma spent every summer and invited each of her five married children and their families in turn to stay with her throughout the summer. Christmas time in 1927 was spent at Grandad's near Sevenoaks in Kent and over Christmas Day and Boxing Day there was a tremendous fall of snow which blocked many roads with snowdrifts, making it impossible for us to drive home to Carshalton in the Morris car.

My father had to get back to the London Stock Exchange and the little branch railway line which ran the four miles or so between the main line at Dunton Green and Westerham was running quite normally. I suppose that's because all trains in that area then were steam-hauled and engines were pretty heavy things, therefore they could grip the rails better and force their way through the drifting snow. Anyway, he had to get to London and we all made for Chevening Halt, half a mile up the road to get the train to Dunton Green and on to London. I was five years old at the time and too small to walk through the deep snow. I have a very clear memory of being carried on the shoulders of one of the men, and I think it was Sid who worked for Grandad, up to the station but I have no recollection at all of the journey itself.

Round about this time Derby Day at Epsom Downs was held on a Wednesday and King George V and Queen Mary used to go there in a large Daimler car on a route which took them along the Beeches Avenue past our house. As I was not at school yet my

10

mother gave me a hand-held Union Jack and stood me on the bank by one of the beech trees and told me to wave it hard when the King's car went by. She shouted, "Here he comes, wave your flag!" and as he went by, sitting in the back seat, I can clearly remember seeing him raise his hat to me because there were very few other people around at that spot and he was sitting on the right-hand side of the seat facing my side of the road. I seem to remember he had a very pointed beard below his chin.

I have already mentioned my late start in going to school and the next eleven years, until I left school at seventeen, were not happy ones. This was due mainly to the fact that I was no good at sport and also found it very difficult to make friends at school. During those middle years my best friend was Stephen who lived on the opposite side of the road to my house and we never even went to the same school. His family moved to Chichester when I was about ten so we used to spend a week at a time at each other's homes during the school holidays. He had two brothers and two sisters and I had none, so it was a complete change for both of us. My main hobby in the early days when he lived over the road was my gauge O Hornby Trains layout which was laid out all over the spare bedroom floor. We compiled full daytime timetables which these trains had to keep to, starting at 7am and finishing at 9pm and Stephen used to come over just before 7am and go just after 9pm. During the day my mother brought us different meals because we could not interrupt the timetable.

At other times Stephen and I would go and stay with my aunt and uncles at the farmhouse near Sevenoaks. Auntie Edie, as she was known, could not have been kinder to us and took us to the cinema at Hastings for the day and seemed to blend in with us so well that we felt just like a threesome. Once Stephen and I went across the fields before sunset on a summer's evening and I felt uneasy because there were cows in the large field and I kept looking all around us. Suddenly on the brow of a bit of a rise I saw what was definitely NOT a cow with its tail in the air and head down coming towards us very fast. Luckily the little branch railway line heading to Westerham was not far off and we succeeded in

11

scrambling through the wire fence on to the railway line just in time, with the bull snorting and panting on the other side of the fence. This meant a longish walk along the track to the nearest station, Chevening Halt. By the time we got there it was nearly dark and several people including the local bobby were out looking for us. This was one of those very rare occasions when Auntie Edie was cross with us.

Roy, one of the men working for my uncles, used to deliver meat in the Morris van to customers over a wide area and Stephen and I would often go with him. There is a particular stretch of road near Seal on the way back to Sevenoaks which is like a switchback and to give us a bit of a thrill he'd race the van down one side and up the other. Each time he did it we'd say, "See if you can go faster than last time!" As a commercial vehicle in those days it was never supposed to travel above 30mph. On one occasion, Roy managed to reach 77mph and we were both so excited when we got back that we told Uncle Char, not realising that we were letting the cat out of the bag by telling him how Roy had broken the law, perhaps dangerously. Uncle Char was good at cricket and golf. When Sam King was the professional at Knole Park Golf Club he would sometimes play with him. In 1934 there was a bi-centenary cricket match held on the Vine Cricket Ground in Sevenoaks where the first match was played in 1734. The players dressed in period costumes and my uncle was one of the umpires. His costume was a brown velvet coat and breeches and three-cornered hat. Two small branches were the wicket with another across the top. The bats were curved and bowling was done underarm. A photo is still held by the Sevenoaks museum and I went to the match with Auntie Edie.

Both of my parents were highly musical. My mother could play any of the popular tunes of the day instantly on the piano, by ear and in any key. My father had a good voice and could tap dance like Fred Astaire. He joined the Stock Exchange Operatic and Dramatic Society in the 1920s and took prominent parts in such shows as 'The Cat's Whiskers', 'No No Nanette', 'The Desert Song' etc which were staged at the Scola Theatre in Charlotte

Street, London. I remember going to see 'The Desert Song' which although I was young seemed to me to be of a very high standard. I've still got some of those early programmes. In one of them, he is seen in top hat, white tie and tails kneeling in the middle of the stage with a bevy of chorus girls on either side of him.

I was much too young at the time to notice but I think my mother had to endure a certain amount of wondering what he got up to during the many rehearsals for these shows. Years later she got her own back because in the 1930s I got measles rather badly and our doctor said I should get some sea air and go to Hastings for a few days. At that time Hastings was in much better shape than it became later on. We stayed at the Queen's Hotel near Hastings Castle; a very good four-star hotel where they changed the sheets every day. One day my mother and I were sitting in the sun lounge at the front of the hotel, and the hall porter in his smart green uniform came in and gave her a note. It said, "Do forgive me for staring at you but I thought you were the Duchess of York", (who later became Queen Elizabeth in 1936) and it was signed "Ernest Marmaduke Ford, Mayor of Hastings". At the bottom of the note he wrote, "I own the Adelphi Hotel in Warrior Square and would be delighted to meet you if you care to telephone me." Well, she did and the next I knew was that he was invited to dinner at our house in Carshalton – and my father was there too.

Many years later after my mother had died and I was clearing out some of her papers I came across several letters from Mr Ford dated at least 12 years after that first meeting. My parents must both have given each other a certain amount of freedom, though I did hear some pretty sharp rows from time to time.

Those early days between the two World Wars must have been very pleasant for those with enough money not to worry about the next pay day. We weren't rich but nearly every house in our road had a live-in maid and many of these came down south from the north of England. Annie, who got twelve shillings and sixpence a week, came from Redcar. She was a good worker but a bit heavy-handed and once she trod on the cat and killed it. Both parents were in great demand because of their musical talents and were always being invited here, there and everywhere. They didn't have to worry about me because Annie lived in and would often keep me amused till bedtime. Likewise, of course, our house was often full of guests who came to dinner or just for a musical evening. I used to hang over the banisters to see who was arriving. I always remember sitting up to have dinner with a particular guest called Freddie Daws, who was also on the Stock Exchange and very wealthy. During conversation he once said, "Do you realise, Frank [my father], one day business people will be able to fly to New York to sign a very important contract and come back the same day to London?" That's exactly what some people did when Concorde was in service over 45 years later. That's like forecasting what travel conditions will be like in 2060 whilst we're in 2014. So he'd certainly got a very good eye on the future in those very early days of international air travel.

By the time I was 9 or 10 years old I was getting very interested in aeroplanes and as we only lived 3 miles from Croydon Aerodrome my father started taking me there on a Sunday morning to see the airliners taking off and arriving from the different capitals of Europe. Croydon had been modernised in 1928 from the earlier primitive place that had grown up after the First World War and the new control tower fascinated me because that's where the newly developing radio equipment was housed and also the Met Office.

Meteorology was to become my overriding interest in life – and still is. I had my first joy flight when I was 10 and remember looking down at our house and seeing everything in the back garden quite clearly. I could even see the tennis balls going to and fro the nets at the local tennis club just up the road.

Round about this time I went to my second school, Barrow Hedges, just 10 minutes' walk from our house. I think my father chose this school because every Sunday a crocodile of around 50 boys passed our house on their way to the parish church for the morning service and they always looked very smart. They were the boarders because the school specialised in taking in children of parents who had overseas jobs in the colonies all over the world. The rest – about 100 – were day boys – and I was one of them. This is where I became aware that I was useless at any sport even though I had won the long jump at my first school. This was where I got my first pair of long trousers, white ones for cricket, but the most I ever scored was 4 runs and I always dropped the catches that came my way.

The main school building was a former country mansion in large grounds and some of the stables had been turned into classrooms, heated by an iron round stove in the middle so that either end of the room was freezing cold in winter time. We always had a film show in the main hall every Saturday evening, chiefly of course for the boarders and there was always an underlying feeling of tension between them and the day boys.

Because I felt so self-conscious about my lack of sporting ability I made no friends at this school during the 3 years I was there which rather blighted my school days. However, when I started having piano lessons with a wonderful teacher, much of my spare time was taken up with practice and over the years I became good enough for my teacher to consider me as a candidate for the Royal College of Music – where she had been a child prodigy.

It may have been due to my lack of enthusiasm for school, but I began to lag behind in the general standard of learning and at the end of this 3-year period I went to Sutton High School for Boys where the school was situated right in the middle of Sutton and had no playing fields. This suited me much better and I started catching up in learning and even made 3 or 4 friends.

During this period, summer holidays always took place at the Wilton Hotel, St Leonards-on-Sea in Sussex. My father used to come down at weekends, usually with 3 or 4 others and as the hotel was unlicensed, they would bring plenty of drink. One evening when things were getting a bit lively one of the bottles became empty and Babe, who was a very playful woman, said, "What shall I do with this bottle?" and my father, not really meaning it, said, "Oh throw it out of the window," which she did

– followed by an almighty crash in the concrete area below. At this, Mr Moore the proprietor came dashing in full of apologies saying, "I'm terribly sorry about the noise, some passing hooligans must have thrown a bottle into my area!" Babe didn't own up.

I was always intrigued to find a very nice elderly lady called Miss Bott still staying at this hotel when we arrived. She'd lived there for several years and had a large mop of grey hair on top of her head like a bird's nest and her bottom teeth overlapped the top ones. She taught me how to make table napkins look like boats with sails and once when I played the short Chopin prelude in C minor to her, she burst into tears.

This was the time I started making my own daily weather records – max. and min. temperatures, barometric pressure, clouds, wind direction and general weather conditions. I wrote all this in an old school physics book; and when I volunteered for the RAF (Royal Air Force) in 1941 this book convinced the Flight Lieutenant Recruiting Officer to put me down as a meteorologist.

Apart from the regular annual visits to the Wilton Hotel, our weekend visits to Grandma's hotel at Worthing meant that we became well known at the Stanhoe Hotel where she stayed. Mrs Beardsal was the chef and I used to hang about the kitchen watching her preparing some of the best food I've ever tasted. She told me she once cooked for the Prince of Wales (who became Edward VIII). Yet in spite of such luxurious meals the full board cost for a week at the Stanhoe was two and a half guineas (£2 12 shillings and 6 pence) in 1934.

Dolly Frankham ran the hotel and her sister kept the bar, leaving Dolly free to take a bit too much gin most nights which she disguised with ginger beer. The bedrooms were very spartan, no en-suite. In fact the chambermaid, Mable, who must have been nearly seventy, used to bring a tall enamel jug full of hot water and stand it outside each bedroom door at about eight o'clock each morning. The floor carpets were rather threadbare and when a strong wind was blowing they would billow up in the middle of the room like a balloon.

16

In spite of such minor details we all used to love staying there. Unfortunately, it was the only hotel on Worthing seafront to be bombed during the Second World War, and no longer exists. I used to keep my max. and min. thermometer in its front garden when I was staying there. I suppose Grandma should have been very happy staying every summer with all her children in succession round her. Perhaps she was, but never once did I ever see her with a smile on her face. Nor do I know how she might sound when she laughed – if ever. All her photographs show a very stern face but I suppose with 8 children she had to be strict to keep them in order. Whenever she gave me any money, usually 10 shillings at birthdays and Christmas, I would say, "Thank you very much," and she would say, "Thank you – what?" I would reply, "Thank you, Grandma, very much," and she'd reply, "That's better." My mother found it very difficult to visit her and even though she only lived 100 yards around the corner, she'd only go there two or three times a year.

Although we nearly always kept a cat I wanted a canary, and in Croydon Market there was a pet shop run by Mr Starling where this canary came from. I remember we asked him if it sang well and he said, "Oh yes, lovely cock bird, it'll sing its head off!" I called it 'Brolo' but it never sang a note. It had some brown feathers among the yellow which suspiciously resembled sparrow feathers and it used to crouch down miserably behind the bottom perch, so much so that I decided as it looked so unhappy that I should find a new home for it with other birds. Fortunately we found someone who lived in Carshalton with quite a big aviary in his garden, and when I took Brolo to his new home I requested that I should return when he had settled down. To all our surprises Brolo had very quickly settled down and built a nest in one of the nestling boxes and laid a couple of eggs! So much for being a singing cock bird.

One of our cats learnt how to knock at the front door and one day as I was coming home from school I caught her in the act. She would reach up on her hind legs as though she were having a good stretch. Then she would hook one of her paws round the knocker, lift it halfway and let it drop. Then she would crouch down and look through the gap at the bottom of the door to see if anyone was there to answer, and if not, she would do it again!

Even at my aunt and uncle's, they always kept a large number of cats because the slaughter house and butcher's shop had to be kept free of rats and mice. The cats were only fed once a day so they did their work very well. At one time there were eleven of them and they all had their own personality. Frizz was born with crumpled-up whiskers and they always stayed like that. Tiddler played games on the farmhouse table with a ping-pong ball which, when thrown to it between the pages of a book standing on edge like a tent it would hit the ball back with its paw and never missed going between the pages. One day, when I was certainly approaching middle age, my aunt said to me, "John, get off that chair, the cat wants it." Sure enough as soon as I stood up the cat DID want it – and got it.

Sunday was the only day of the week when my uncles had any time to themselves and Uncle Char was quite musical and could play simple tunes on the piano. He would sit in the room known as the 'Little Room' and listen to records from musical shows. One day before he came in the room I was playing the Debussy piece 'Gardens in the Rain' and as he walked past the door he put his head round it and said, "You can stop that noise, Johnny." I've been told that when I was much younger, I was sitting with him and when he went to change the record I said, "When is the dirge going to start, Uncle Char?" referring to his piano playing. Where I learnt that word no-one seems to know. My aunt had a very effective way of lighting the fire in that room. She would collect some red hot embers from the kitchen range in a big shovel and run along the passage to the fireplace and throw them onto some dry wood in the grate and in no time there was a roaring fire there.

I was never very fond of my name John because it sounded so abrupt, unlike two-syllable words like David, Peter and Richard and so on. Because there were so many male relatives, John apparently was the only popular name that had not been used when I came along. When I was very young my mother called me

"Sweetie" but soon realised this was not at all suitable. So she shortened it to "Swet" and this stuck for quite a few years with the occasional "Duck" thrown in. My father on the other hand loved funny sounding words such as "staggering catfish" which he shortened to "Stag" or sometimes he'd change it to "Vin". In the Air Force because I had naturally blond hair it was inevitable I became "Blondie". Even the Italian family I got to know in Sicily in 1944 called me that. My own choice for a name would have been "Tony" not realising that I was quite entitled to be called that because my second name is "Anthony". They do say, "What's in a name?" But it's quite strange how often you see people who have names that seem to suit their looks.

I've inherited my father's liking for funny words and when Laos was in the news, its capital city, Luang Prabang always amused me. But what is most strange is that my cousin in Vancouver, whom I've visited 4 or 5 times has exactly the same peculiar sense of humour and had even chosen Luang Prabang for one of his pet words.

All through my school days we had the usual photo taken of the whole school in 4 or 5 tiers but I always felt unhappy with the way I looked in them – always very solemn and not nearly as good looking as most of the other boys around me. Then as adolescence approached I was landed with a new burden of horrid spots and boils all round the back of my neck, but fortunately not often on my face, and this scourge lasted a full 10 years and didn't finally clear up until my mid 20s. Going to the barbers was always a problem because it cut away a lot of hair that was hiding the spots. No wonder I was such a shy, withdrawn, unattractive teenager.

My final school was Epsom College, and when I was about to take the Common Entrance exam I got measles and couldn't take it. Yet my father managed to persuade the Head Master that if they sent my day-to-day papers from Sutton High School to Epsom and they were found to be satisfactory, would he consider that to be good enough? Surprisingly, he did, so I got in without having taken the exam.

19

As a day boy, life became very full with homework, piano practice and school on Saturdays till 5 or 6 pm. There were about 350 boarders and 150 day boys, and in retrospect I think life would have been much better as a boarder rather than a day boy. For one thing, the boarders got to know most of the masters in out-of-school activities such as the debating society, poetry readings, stamp collecting etc, usually in the masters' private quarters. My Latin master was a big man who made me feel very uneasy, such as the day I had to stand up and read in Latin from one of the books. As I struggled with the strange words he interrupted me in a very loud voice and said, "Sit down, you creature of darkest night!" Years later, when I met him at an Old Boys' meeting, he was hosting the tea party and I was sitting right next to him. This time he was a bit shy with me but I quickly realised what an extremely nice man he was. As a boarder, I would probably already have found that out.

Life at Epsom College had great emphasis on all sporting activities and every afternoon from Monday to Saturday was devoted to some sport or other. The only thing I was any good at was cross-country running and in fact I was in the Crawfurd Junior Cross-Country Team which suited me very well because when the ground was too hard to play rugger in cold weather, we always went on a cross-country run instead.

One of the most memorable events during these school years occurred in the summer holidays of 1938 when my father took me to Paris for the weekend from Croydon Airport in an Imperial Airways airliner known as the 'Hannibal' Class. It was a Handley Page HP 42 large bi-plane that carried 38 passengers in supreme luxury at a stately 95–100 miles per hour. The journey took two and a half hours and because airliners weren't pressurised in those days, we flew at about 5,000 feet which meant you could see much detail on the ground. I remember on the return journey as we flew over Hastings we could see Mrs Davidson's (who came with us) house in St Helen's Down Road near Alexandra Park. I was looking forward to testing my French while I was in Paris but during the whole weekend I only uttered one word, *"Troisième"* when the lift boy asked me *"Quel étage Monsieur?"*

When we arrived on the Friday evening during dinner we were asked if we'd like to go on a 'Paris by Night' tour which we did. It started at around 11pm and one of the ports of call was a small hall shaped like an underground tunnel where we sat near some heavy curtains. There was a bottle of champagne on the table which cost the equivalent of two shillings. After a short while there was a drum roll behind these curtains which parted to reveal a line of dancing girls with nothing on but a few feathers. Very soon they ended their dancing and came down the steps either side of the stage. One of them came and sat on my knee with her arm around my neck, much to my father's amusement.

I think possibly my parents were aware how much I disliked going to school and they may have thought that if I became a boarder this would give me more spare time and perhaps make one or two friends. But at the mere suggestion of it I can clearly remember saying, "If you make me a boarder, I shall run away." Looking at the idea from a completely different perspective I'm pretty sure they were right.

On Founders Day in 1937 I was standing with my parents watching the cricket match and nearby were two boys, Bennett and Gordon, who were in my class. They were inseparable pals and I was secretly envious of their close friendship especially as they were both very good looking. After Gordon had been talking to me for a short while and they moved away, my father said something to the effect that they seemed a very nice couple – and perhaps hinting that I ought to try and make a similar friendship with someone which, for some deep-seated reason, I found impossible.

When the School Certificate Exams came along I did better than expected especially in Maths, Physics, Chemistry and French so would certainly have been well placed for the 6th Form in the following school year, but that was not to be.

21

St. Hilda's – Miss Moore is holding my arm, 1928.

'Not the only pebble on the beach' at St. Leonards.

My first pair of long trousers.

Group school photo at Barrow Hedges School, 1931–1934.

Imperial Airways HP 42 airliner in which I flew to Paris in 1938.

Epsom College Junior Cross-Country Team 1937 –
I am in the back row (left).

Carshalton Beeches Railway Bridge before widening.

Carshalton Beeches Railway Bridge after widening.

CHAPTER 3

RAF

This was 1939 and instead of going back to school that September my father decided I should leave prematurely and start work in the local Lloyds Bank (arranged by our next door neighbour who was the manager of Lloyds Bank, Carshalton) which I did on 2nd October 1939. I don't really know why he did this because the school opened normally even though the Second World War had started on 3rd September 1939. It may have been something to do with the fact that my father was on the Officers' Emergency Reserve and was already in the army by February 1940 when I would be nearly 18, and so becoming liable for serving in the forces myself. I was nevertheless denied what most people say is the best year of all during your school days when you are in the 6th Form because that is when you begin to realise that school teachers are human after all and also start to treat you in a more adult manner as well.

Life as a Junior Bank Clerk in 1939 was totally manual. Statements were handwritten and each page added up without the benefit of anything to check it with except on 'balance day' once a fortnight. Then every penny had to be accounted for. Ledgers were huge, very heavy loose-leaf affairs and the customer's name was written with pen and black ink in copperplate writing.

When the air raids started in 1940 I took my turn in doing fire-watching duties once or twice a week. My colleagues for this were Miss Thain who ran the tobacconist and sweet shop next to the bank and Mr Bennell who was the fishmonger and had a shop just past Miss Thain's. We used to meet at around 8pm and go down to the basement of the Joint Electricity Authority's showroom on the other side of the road. We'd take it in turns to do two-hour watchkeeping while the other two got as much rest as possible because at the end of the night at about 6 or 7am we'd all go home, have a bath and breakfast and do a normal day's work.

The manager of our bank was Mr Beeching and his elder son Tony was a child actor of about 15. He was in the film *Goodbye Mr Chips* with Robert Donat. Tony was in the scene when he's in a railway carriage sitting opposite Robert Donat. He also did a lot of voice commercials for Radio Luxembourg and Radio Normandie. Unfortunately he had a very severe form of diabetes and died before he was 20. Besides being a bank manager Mr Beeching and his wife ran a pub at Seal in Kent and every day, in spite of petrol rationing, managed to cover the 20 or so miles to the bank in his car. This of course was in the early days of the war before rationing of all kinds became very much more tightly controlled.

I was taught the main course of my duties by a very pleasant 27-year-old called Gerald Norris. Gerald had been left a small fortune some years earlier by a rich uncle and simply worked at the bank for something to do. He was one of the first 30,000 or so people in Greater London to own a television set when the BBC started the first regular TV service in the world in November 1936. He had a very funny made-up word for pound notes which I can't spell but it sounded like "Jilliogoblins". When I left the bank to join the RAF he gave me a very nice wristwatch which I decided was too good to wear in the forces. I carried on wearing the watch my father had given me 4 years previously, which I've still got in working order. The good watch was stolen during the war when the house was being repaired after bomb damage.

The time soon came round when my age group was due to be called up but I decided if I volunteered I might stand a better chance of becoming a meteorologist which is what I desperately wanted to be. I went to Sutton Labour Exchange while I was still 18 and said I wanted to volunteer for the RAF, which was noted and they told me I'd be notified where to go in due course. Three months later I was told to report to an address in Croydon in July 1941. My father was then stationed in Bury St Edmunds so he managed to get time off on that date and came with me to Croydon.

Looking back on those events it must have been a very hard blow for my mother to be deserted by her husband and only son on the same day and I've never really known what she did when we both left the house because I know my father had to return to his unit.

About 30 of us, all around 20 years old were taken to RAF Cardington near Bedford from Croydon that first night. It was the first time I had slept in the same hut with so many complete strangers from all different walks of life. What a shock! Some with cockney-like accents told dirty stories in the dark; others were quietly talking to their neighbours. I was lying still in the dark, not having anything to say to anyone but eventually dropping off to sleep. Next day we still got dressed in our civilian clothes but were given our Service Number (1453120) and interviewed by a Flight Lieutenant to decide what trade we would like to do in the RAF. When I said I wanted to be a meteorologist, he replied, "Oh you can't do that because we take all our Met men fully trained from the Air Ministry." At which, I said, "But you must!" and promptly brought out my (quite impressive) meteorological records and statistics which I had maintained on a daily basis since I was 12 in 1935. He was suitably impressed and I can't think how I'd had the presence of mind to bring these records with me when I left home. After a brief look at the pages of calculations, graphs, and weather reports, the Flight Lieutenant said, "Just a minute." He must have gone off to see his Superior Officer and within quite a short time came back and said, "OK, we'll take you in as a meteorologist and send you to the Met Training School at Gloucester."

What a stroke of luck that was. Soon afterwards we were measured and issued with a uniform and full set of underclothes and shoes (not boots). Square-bashing (initial training) followed for 4 weeks and we were carted off to Great Yarmouth for this. At the end of it all we were lined up and told where our next posting would be for whatever trade we'd been given. I knew I should be sent to Gloucester but when my name was called out they said, "To Blackpool." I went straight to the Orderly Room and asked why I was being sent to Blackpool. I was told that all motorcyclists were trained there. Apparently the WAAF (Women's Auxiliary Air Force) who registered my number and trade couldn't spell meteorologist and her scribbled efforts had been read as motorcyclist. At that moment a Squadron Leader Padre walked through the Orderly Room and I grabbed his arm saying, "Please can you help me?" telling him what had happened. He very kindly said he'd see what he could do and the upshot was that my posting was cancelled but I had to do the square-bashing all over again while they put the records straight.

While I was at Great Yarmouth my father, who was now a Captain, was not far away at Bury St Edmunds and one Sunday he came over to take me out to lunch. When he got to the Guard Room the Duty Sergeant came to where I was living (a row of terraced houses) to collect me. On the way he said to me, "Even though he is your father you must salute him when you meet."

Now this is a very strange example of how coming events cast their shadows. Many years earlier when I was about 7 or 8, I had been given a bus conductor's toy uniform complete with peak cap and ticket machine. When my father saw me with this cap on (about 1929) it must have reminded him of officers' caps at the end of the First World War and so he showed me the correct way to salute, just 12 years before I was now doing it for real.

My father had come over from Bury St Edmunds to take me out to lunch in one of the few hotels still operating on Great Yarmouth seafront. He was based in Rushbrooke Hall, home of Lord Rothschild and part of which had been taken over by the army to house a fleet of military ambulances. One day quite an extraordinary event took place. Not far away there was an EFTS (Elementary Flying Training School) just outside Cambridge using Tiger Moths and as one of them was flying over Rushbrooke Hall it developed engine trouble and found a clear area in the grounds to make an emergency landing. The instructor and his pupil jumped out and my father hurried over to meet them and make sure they were alright. Imagine their surprise when the pupil turned out to be Graham King, the school boy who used to call at our house every morning 10 years earlier so we could both go to school together. Poor Graham was killed in a completely needless way a few months later when he was based at Kidlington near Oxford and went up on a test flight as a passenger in a Handley Page Hamden bomber which crashed and killed them all on board.

One of the tantalising things about our training marches northwards along Great Yarmouth seafront was that in those days the makers of Smiths Crisps had a factory just the other side of the road from the seafront and invariably the westerly wind would blow the appetising smell of the cooking crisps right at us as we turned round and marched back to our less than appetising lunch. Also during our rifle training we were taken to the range for some firing practice and the instructor said, "The person with the top score gets 48 hours' leave." That was me, but I never got the leave. What I did get was much better a little later on; a posting to the Met Training School at Gloucester.

We were billeted in private houses and I was with a family of a mother and her teenage daughter and the mother's 38-year-old brother whose bedroom I shared. Fortunately he did not snore but in any case I used to hitchhike back home on Saturday afternoons and get a late train on Sunday nights out of Paddington arriving at my digs at about 1am.

Looking back on those days I never once spent any time looking around Gloucester. What a pity, I should have done. I shall always remember my first day at the Training School. It was in September and quite a bright sunny morning. The instructor said to us (about 25 of us in all), "I want you all to go outside and then come in and tell me what you've seen." I went out and had a look at a lot of blue sky with several clouds and clear visibility. There was a gentle breeze but I had no idea which direction it was blowing from. But when the instructor said, "What sort of clouds were they?" I didn't know how they were divided up into different categories in spite of my years of record-keeping. Then he went on to describe the 3 main types – Low, Medium and High clouds and in each category there are at least 9 different types; I was completely bowled over. To me, the sky had always been just blue or cloudy.

The course lasted just over 4 weeks and one of the skills you had to develop was how to use 2 pens tied together; one for black ink and the other for red, because when drawing a weather map, each station's weather report has to be drawn with some of the items in black and others in red. This of course was long before computers took over.

I was very impressed when the instructor was explaining the THEN method of sending out weather reports by means of a 5-group, 5-figure system. He said this was the only truly universal system that could be understood by all languages throughout the world, a remarkable fact which I think deserves to be described here in some detail. It is now nearly 70 years since I plotted a weather map using these numbers, so as I only had my memory to rely on, the results may not be 100% perfect.

When I was based in England, the weather maps we used were of the British Isles and surrounding sea areas and a typical weather report from Croydon Aerodrome might look something like this:

15126, 25644, 24467, 99696, 83504 when plotted on the weather map would look like this:

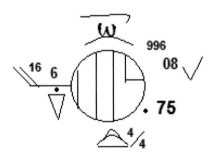

Some of the detail would be in red ink but we cannot show that here. This is a fairly late April typical weather situation. There is a large amount of information in this plot as can be seen from the meaning of all the numbers listed on the next page.

1st Group 15126	
1	Country of origin 1= UK. (Secret during WW2 but neutrals, e.g. 3 = Spain, were broadcast worldwide)
51	Station identity 51 = Croydon.
2	Type of low cloud 2 = large cumulus
6	Type of medium cloud 6 = alto cumulus spread out from tops of large cumulus
2nd Group 25644	
25	Present weather 25 = showers of rain
6	Visibility 6 = 4 – 6 miles
4	Amount of low cloud 4 = 4/10 of the sky covered
4	Height of low cloud's base above station 4 = 600 – 1000 feet
3rd Group 24467	
24	Wind direction 24 = due west
4	Wind speed 4 = 10 -13 m.p.h.
6	Past weather since previous observation 6 = rain
7	Total cloud cover 7 = almost completely covered, but some gaps of blue sky
4th Group 99616	
996	Barometric pressure corrected to sea level 996 MBS = 'Change' on Home Barometers
16	Temperature in centigrade 16 C = 61 F
5th Group 83504	
8	Relative humidity 8 = around 75%, which is high
3	Type of high cloud 3 = anvil cirrus – seen in thundery skies
504	Tendency, Barometer change since previous observation 504 = falling then rising

The other activity which was new to me was using a theodolite to track a large balloon as it rose filled with hydrogen at a known rate. As the balloon was being filled it had a certain weight attached to it so that when the gas reached a precise volume, the uplift balanced the weight and the balloon remained stationary in the air so that when the weight was removed the balloon would rise at 500 feet per minute. In this way you could work out what the wind speed and direction was at various levels right up to perhaps 20,000 feet. At that height there was another way of finding the wind speed and direction by using a nephoscope. This was like a garden rake on the end of a long pole with the spikes at the top of the pole against the sky. When you saw a suitable piece of cirrus cloud (not any of the other types), you would line it up with one of the spikes and time it till it reached the next spike, at the same time twisting the pole so that the piece of cloud was in the same relative position as it was with the first spike. With a dial near the bottom of the pole with 360 degrees on it there were tables worked out that told you what the wind speed and direction was at 20,000 feet. One of our forecasters in Sicily loved doing this and would suddenly say, "I think I'll go outside for a bit of quiet nephing."

When I completed the Met Training course in October 1941, I had hoped that I would be sent to an airfield but my first posting was to an army unit based near Bishop's Stortford using the buildings of the evacuated Felsted School. As we were a small RAF unit working with a large army group, we were billeted separately and housed in the local vicarage. One day the elderly sister of the vicar asked me if I could see what was wrong with her bedside radio. Although I told her I was no expert in radios I had a look at it for her. Much to my surprise it was an old crystal set very similar to the one I had at home which my father bought in 1925 and which still works to this day. All that was wrong with it was the aerial wire had slipped out of its socket. I put it back and on came the programme. At which she said, "Oh you are so clever!"

At this time, around the new year of 1942, we had to take part in an army exercise sleeping in army huts and on one very cold January night I took off my wet boots and put them on the floor beside my bed. Next morning they were frozen to the floor. During the spring of that year I was able to come home for 36 hours between the end of a spell of night shifts and my next daytime duty. As I got home on this occasion I felt quite ill with a very high temperature. Our doctor called to see me and immediately diagnosed scarlet fever. He bundled me off straight away to the isolation hospital where I found myself the only adult in a ward full of children. I was soon an item of interest for them all and when my mother came to see me they all called out, "Mr John, your mum's here to see you!"

I was away from my unit for about 4 weeks, at the end of which the RAF Medical Officer at Croydon Aerodrome (now a fighter-base) finally signed me off as fit for duty.

At the end of 1942 I was sent on embarkation leave and finally left Greenock at the end of November in a convoy of about 40 vessels of different kinds on board a beautiful ship called the *Reina Del Pacifico* which was packed full of army personnel. I was able to ring my father just before we sailed and this proved to be the last time I was to speak to him. The reason being that I remained overseas until May 1946 and he died in March 1945 with a tumour on the brain, aged 49.

By coincidence we landed at Algiers on 6th December 1942 which was his birthday. Just three months earlier we had both been able to get 7 days' leave at the same time. So to make the most of it my parents and I spent a very pleasant 5 days at our favourite hotel in Torquay. In retrospect this has more poignancy both for me and my mother because we were all never to be together again on such an occasion.

Even in 1942, one of the darkest years of the whole war for Britain, Torquay had a remarkably peaceful atmosphere and you were only reminded of the war by columns of aircrew under training as they marched along the seafront wearing their forage caps with the white flash that indicated what they would be doing in the near future. Casualty rates were extremely high once the bombing campaign really got under way but young people are notoriously optimistic which is why they can take such risks as Fighter or Bomber Crews.

I've always looked younger than I really was so I didn't feel like a shirker in my civilian clothes on holiday because I was really only just above school age.

The voyage to North Africa had taken us in a wide sweep out into the Atlantic as the U-boats were causing a lot of damage at that time but I remember the thrilling feeling as we passed through the Strait of Gibraltar and seeing the brightly lit towns on the southern side after 3 years of blackout in the UK.

Although the ship was full of army personnel, we 15 meteorologists were the only RAF people on board so we were very lucky to have a large cabin with double bunks all to ourselves. The sun seemed to shine for most of the voyage and I spent a lot of time sunbathing on deck, quite oblivious to the deadly danger that was probably trying to get at us. Meal times were a bit of a scramble but I did enjoy the white bread after the UK's monotonous brown bread. I always felt very envious of the officers who were travelling in First Class comfort and having very civilised meals and being waited on in the elegant dining room. I have always felt that in this respect the gulf between the way officers live and those who are not officers is too great in the British Military Forces. But in the case of the US Forces they've gone too far the other way.

Once we set foot in North Africa I was so excited to be in the Mediterranean area that I found a small bottle and went on to the beach to fill it with seawater and sent it home saying, "This is the Mediterranean Sea", and they got it!

From the very start of my Met Training Course in Gloucester I felt very much at home with my fellow students. We all had the required qualifications in Maths and Physics and indeed the forecasters who were all officers had to have degrees in these subjects. Because of this, many of the wartime forecasters had been school masters in civilian life and as such were used to dealing with younger people. This meant that being on duty with the forecaster became a very relaxed affair as we got to know one another. I spent many hours of duty with our senior forecaster who was a squadron leader talking about music and our likes and dislikes of composers. Throughout the five and a half years which I spent in the RAF I enjoyed the company of my colleagues and continued friendships made during that time right up to the present day.

My lasting regret was that I could not become a forecaster and officer because I lacked the necessary degrees. I loved being a meteorologist and did not want to leave met work in order to become an officer in some other occupation. So I had to accept the fact that I would remain in the ranks for the rest of the war. In retrospect, this did not turn out to be such a bad thing because I ended up having the best year of my life on a Flying Boat base in Sicily from which I returned to the UK in May 1946 to be demobilised a few weeks later.

The war years overseas from 1942–1946 did provide some interesting and at times uncomfortable experiences. My first posting in North Africa was to a delightful town in the hilly country well to the east of Algiers called Constantine. It was very French in character and we lived in civilised barracks near the centre of the town. We were attached to the 1st Army HQ, and off duty got to know two English ladies who had been there as missionaries for some years living in the Arab quarter. They invited us to their house whenever we had the time to relax and listen to the BBC overseas service but I nearly always felt dreadfully homesick when Big Ben was striking.

On Christmas Day 1942, I was on duty from 1pm – 8pm with a break at 6pm for the traditional Christmas dinner, served by the officers, as is the custom in the British Forces. This was the first time I had been served wine and did not know anything about the effects it can have. Consequently I drank too much and staggered back to the remains of my duty which included drawing the 1800 hours weather map. Next morning they showed me the map; a spider could have made a much better job of it.

A few days later an invitation was received from a French family for any two airmen who might be off duty to visit them on New Year's Eve. Roy Howe and I were the lucky ones chosen and all the family with several children were waiting for us. They had gone to immense trouble gathering interesting items of food which was very scarce for them, but we spent the whole time having little courses of many varieties until it was time to leave. Some days later Roy and I returned to say thank you to them with a tin of corned beef we'd got from the cookhouse. It was pitiful to see just how barren their daily life must have been because gone were all the decorations etc. from the day of the party. Nevertheless the corned beef was about the best thing we could have given them.

Shortly after this we were on the move again, this time being billeted in school buildings in a very hilly district not far from Souk Ahras. It was here that, as I learnt later, a strange thing happened. This school was quite close to a very steep hillside and when I was off duty during the daytime, I used to walk up the grassy slopes of this hill in the pleasantly warm winter sunshine and find a comfortable spot away from all the crowds to write letters. At this time my mother was living in Bury St Edmunds near to where my father was stationed. One Sunday, out of curiosity, she went to a spiritualist church and after the service several people stayed behind to listen to a talk by a medium. When my mother spoke to her the medium said, "Have you a son called John?" (a very common name so nothing unusual about that). Then she went on to say, "He is in blue [RAF colour] and I can see him sitting on a mountain side and he is writing to you." And I never ever saw anyone else doing the same thing.

Our next move took place in early March 1943 when the days were quite warm but cold at night, but now we were under canvas with 8 to each tent. This style of living was destined to last for nearly a year. Each morning you had to be careful before putting on your boots that a scorpion hadn't crept inside overnight and although there was a lot of rain before the hot dry weather set in, a good wash and shower was something we all longed for.

38

My 21st birthday was celebrated – if that's the right word – under such conditions and I vowed then to have a big 31st party instead, which I did.

An unusual episode happened at the beginning of May 1943 when 6 of us were sent to a lighthouse at Cap Ferrat just west of Bizerte. We were there to report weather conditions and shared the place with the then Secret Radar Unit. Suddenly one day we realised we were the target for a lone FW 190 aircraft which was preparing to dive-bomb us. As it dived towards us, I crouched under the radar vehicle only to realise I was right beside the explosive that was only to be used if the vehicle was in immediate danger of being captured. Fortunately for all of us the single bomb just missed the cliff top on which we stood and dropped harmlessly into the sea several hundred feet below – the closest shave probably of the whole war. I have since sailed past that lighthouse on a couple of occasions on cruises and as I've gazed through my binoculars at the headland with its well-known lighthouse, I've always had a sort of revived feeling of terror.

Shortly after returning to our base at 1st Army HQ, the Afrika Corps, trapped in the Cap Bon Peninsula surrendered and all fighting in North Africa ceased. The effect in those first few days was dramatic because huge numbers of German soldiers were now Prisoners of War and on that first day of their captivity we had to sit down with some of them in the mess tent at supper time. We found ourselves sitting opposite some very forlorn men but still looking smart in their tropical kit. At that moment I couldn't help feeling sorry for them and the thought occurred to me that just the day before, our respective duties were to kill each other. Looking at them now I thought how decent they looked and I would have rather been friends with them because they looked so like ourselves.

Our final move took us to Carthage, and the floor of my tent had traces of Roman mosaics. As we were near the sea, daily bathing was a regular luxury except one day while I was in the water my clothes were stolen and all I had was a towel around my waist with which to return to the camp.

Winston Churchill paid us a visit on 1st June 1943 and in Tunis ENSA (Entertainments National Service Association) put on a show which included Leslie Henson. These days of relaxation were short-lived because the next operation was the invasion of Sicily in July 1943. Once ashore we set up camp just outside Syracuse. One of our officers, Flt Lt B. P. Clode, had been a school master and he managed to get an army vehicle to take several of us who were off duty to visit the Greek amphitheatre and other ancient remains.

At the end of August I finally got the posting I'd been longing for, after a 2-year delay, to an aerodrome in western Sicily, leaving army units for good. A lorry was provided for several airmen and our officer (Flt Lt Clode) to take us across the island (it's the biggest one in the Med) to an airfield near a village called Bo Rizzo which is between Marsala and Trapani. We covered 123 miles on the first day over quite good roads but very hilly and twisty. That night I cooked the supper for the whole party of 9 on the beach near Licata. I can remember sleeping on the tailboard of the lorry, parked near the murmuring waves, looking up at the brilliant stars above me and thinking what a fantastic experience this was, especially as the whole group got on very well and were like a bunch of friends on a camping holiday. The second night was spent in similar but not quite so idyllic circumstances and that afternoon we passed a banana grove and I had my first taste of bananas for 4 years.

After setting up the tents on arrival at the airfield we discovered that apart from Beaufighters there was a section of American Dakotas on the other side of the field and so we had the very good US rations that were provided for them. Here for the first time since leaving the UK I was able to pay a local Sicilian to do my laundry for me instead of struggling with it myself. The currency was cigarettes because as a non-smoker the free issue of 50 per week was quite useful for bartering. Once or twice a week a lorry was provided to take us to the beach for a swim.

In November I had to go to the RAF hospital with jaundice and remained in there for a week. Conditions were pretty poor; no glass in the windows, double-deck beds made of canvas and a strict diet of no fat and not much else. A few days after I recovered I hitchhiked a lift on my day off in one of the Dakotas going to Palermo for the day, arriving just after 9am and getting back to base at 4.15pm. Then in December I did the same thing only this time to Tunis where I met one of my colleagues from the time we were at Felsted School. I had difficulty when I tried to return and had to go to Palermo for the night and on to my home base next morning arriving in time to go on duty at 1pm. I certainly wouldn't take such risks now if I knew I had to be on duty the next day. Just one week later, the officer I'd been on the night duty with asked if I'd like to go with him on another Dakota trip, first to Catania, then on to Malta, then back the same way, in time for tea. This trip sticks in my memory because between Catania and Malta the pilot flew so low we had to climb in order to clear a ridge of hills to the south of Catania. It was very thrilling. At this time we had a motor cycle which belonged to the section and one of my colleagues who could drive, took me on the pillion to the hill-top village of Erice, 2300 feet high which dominates the surrounding countryside. I remember the cups in a restaurant up there had the German Swastika on the underside, so it may have been an officers' mess before the Sicilian invasion.

Life at Bo Rizzo was by no means dull, especially as I made off-duty flights to Tunis, Catania and Malta, apart from another 9 days in hospital with suspected glandular fever. Trapani and Mount Erice were interesting places to visit for the occasional meal.

What did come as a surprise in February 1944 was to be given leave at the Mt. Etna rest camp – a very modern hotel situated 6,000 feet up on the slopes of the volcano amidst deep snow. One evening I volunteered to play the piano to a packed ballroom and even though I had not touched a piano since leaving the UK, I think I gave a reasonable performance of Chopin's 'Fantasie Impromptu in C sharp minor' and Rachmaninoff's 'Prelude', also in C sharp minor. I've no idea how I managed to do such a thing with no chance to practise beforehand – I don't even remember feeling nervous. I suppose that's one of the advantages of being 21.

As is so often the case in military affairs, as soon as I returned to Bo Rizzo after my leave – a very long journey – I got a posting all the way back over the same route to the aerodrome at Catania where I arrived just 2 weeks after I'd spent the 7 days' leave just up the road on Mt. Etna.

Now, for the first time for over a year, I was no longer under canvas but living in some considerable comfort just behind Catania Cathedral in a commandeered building, the Palazzo Biscari. Civilisation at last! The YMCA was in a building in the heart of the town and the main street, Via Etnea, had a wonderful shop called Pasticceria Svizzera where we could buy the Sicilian speciality ice cream called Cassata. I also found a room where I could do some piano practice. When we were on duty we had a lorry which took us the 3 miles to the aerodrome, passing on the way an enormous cemetery. Italian cemeteries are most interesting places but never once did I go in there. I wish now that I had done so.

My joy at being sent to Catania was further increased because I linked up again with Tommy Hatton with whom, on and off, I spent most of the three and a half years we were overseas together. Tommy was the son of a Welsh coal miner from Mountain Ash and he had the ability to darn socks more neatly than anyone else I ever knew. We became close pals and spent days off together hitchhiking to places like Noto and Avola. When I started making a model glider it was Tommy that flew it one day and crashed it – but it soon got mended. Once, I called him Thomas and he said, "No – that's not my name, my parents christened me Tom because they said that is what most people will call you for the rest of your life."

Catania is only about 50 minutes by train from the famous and beautiful tourist attraction of Taormina and this is where I met the Varaschini family – an English lady married to a very clever Italian engineer with a 17-year-old daughter Patricia (Pat) and a 14-year-old son – Carlo (Sonny). These people more or less dominated my off-duty days for the rest of my time (2 years) in Sicily. Pat and I are still in touch as I write this in 2012.

A year of work and play in Catania led to the saddest day of my young life – 5th March 1945. That is the date my father died back in London when he was only 49 and a major in the RASC (Royal Army Service Corps. I'd had no idea he was seriously ill with a tumour on the brain so it was almost 2 weeks after his death that I got a sympathy letter from a friend. As the war was still on in Europe, I had no chance of getting any compassionate leave and had to cope with the blow as best I could, as it was going to be another 15 months before I did return to the UK for good.

I have repeatedly noticed that it seems to be a strange fact that life is full of compensations because no sooner had I received the bad news, I was given other news which was a posting together with Tom Hatton from Catania to a flying boat base to the south of Catania called Augusta, just short of Syracuse. Here I was to stay almost for exactly another year and I can say without any hesitation, that year has proved to be the best year of my whole life. There I made several life-long friends and we lived in very comfortable pre-war Italian naval shore establishments; the natural harbour was delightful for bathing, tennis and cricket. The flying boats were so different from land planes and every landing and take-off was something to be watched; and the Varaschinis and others also in Taormina were only two and half hours away by train. Also, I was more dedicated to meteorology than ever. Shall I go on? No, there were other delights, but I might become boring.

Other close friends I met at Augusta were Jim Carlile, who slept in the bunk above mine, and Eric Thomson who had been a diamond sorter with De Beers before joining the RAF. We all shared the same room which overlooked the cricket pitch and bathing beach behind. Jim and I once hired a tandem bicycle to go to Syracuse and he always blamed me for sitting on the back seat because he said he had to do all the work. Anyway, we got to Syracuse but were both so tired we put the bike on the train and came back in comfort. Eric tried to teach me how to play bridge, but I never got the hang of it because I was not really interested.

43

He always got cross with me when I played an ace which at that point was not really necessary. Both of these friends have now sadly died, but we all kept in touch right to the very end.

One night when I was on night duty, the pilot used to come to the Met Office for a route forecast at about 5am before an early take-off for the flight to Poole Harbour. I always took my writing paper on duty to write home in the short period between weather observations (every hour) and drawing weather maps and so for the rest of the time my writing case was in a haversack hung over the back of my chair. One day, two or three of the flying boat crew came in and when they left, one of them mistook my haversack for his own. After they left I discovered what had happened and as we shared the office with Air Traffic Control, they were still in radio range and could receive our message to return it. Unfortunately on the way back from England the new crew forgot to unload it at Augusta so my writing case went on to the next stopping place which was Cairo. Another radio message got it on another return flight and this time I did get it back.

Very often the passengers included entertainers either going out or returning from entertaining the forces in the far corners of the world and I always remember Paula Green who was a well-known singer with bands like Geraldo's, who gave us a full concert before going to bed for an early start next morning.

It was only 6 months after I arrived at Augusta that I was again surprised to learn I was going to be given 2 weeks' leave, but this time back home in the UK after an absence of 3 years. Tommy Hatton was also going to travel with me and the journey was going to take nearly 10 days. First of all, we got on a destroyer at Catania to go to Malta and before we even left the quayside one of the WRENS (Women's Royal Naval Service) on board was seasick even though there were no waves in sight.

I think because the journey by flying boat to the UK only took about 8 hours it is probably worth quoting from my diary just how we took so long to cover the same distance by land and sea. So here are the details:

6/11/1945	Set off for Catania
7/11/1945	Left Catania by sea for Malta. Slept at Nuffield House
8/11/1945	Had a look round Valetta and did some shopping. Spent another night here
9/11/1945	Left aboard 'Stefan Batory', a Polish ship, (for Toulon)
10/11/1945	Felt ill in rough sea, but not sick. The ship's black cat looked green and had been sick
11/11/1945	Sea still rough, but arrived Toulon, (war damaged) at 2pm, and got train with LNER coaches but French electric locomotive and started at 10.30pm. While waiting in the siding, the P.L.M. 'Train Bleu' passed through very slowly and we could see the Champagne bottles and rich food in the restaurant cars – 1945!
12/11/1945	Reached Bram just beyond Toulouse and got out of the train for breakfast and general wash and brush up. Travelled all day and got out again for supper. On again through the night.
13/11/1945	Hardly slept during the train journey and arrived at Dieppe at middle day. Cross channel sailed at 11.30pm.
14/11/1945	Arrived at Newhaven at 6am got to London at 10.30am. Tommy and I both needed a good soak in a hot bath which took the rest of the morning. As Tommy had never been to London before, I took him to Paddington for his train to South Wales. I couldn't bring myself to go home for the first time in 3 years until the 4.38pm train and I suppose that reluctance to return home for the first time after such a long gap was because I was going to see my mother for the first time as a widow. It certainly showed on her face when I did first meet her but one soon becomes used to different circumstances.

The 14 days' leave passed all too quickly and the return to Augusta was very similar to the homeward journey. Life soon resumed its regular pattern except Jim was made a sergeant and so went to live in different quarters. I missed his company but we could still make our off-duty trips to Taormina together.

When Christmas time came, the usual tradition of the officers serving the men with their Christmas dinners took place and our Commanding Officer was Sqd/Ldr Fry. When he put my dinner in front of me I was able to ask him quite politely if he was anything to do with the famous 'Fry's Chocolate Cream' to which he replied, "Oh, yes, I am part of the family that runs the Fry's Chocolate Company in Bristol." He used to fly a Walrus Amphibian seaplane which could be used for Air Sea Rescue purposes if needed, but when Sqd/Ldr Fry used it, he had two reasons for doing so. One was to let out the water that leaked into the hull once he got into the air, and the second was to nip up to Catania and bring back a load of extras for the Officers' Mess.

Once the New Year started, my days at Augusta rapidly drew to an end and in May 1946 I was repatriated to the UK prior to final demobilisation in August. I had hoped I might go home in one of the flying boats but they were usually too fully booked for me to do so. I therefore had to make that tedious journey for the third time.

My final months in the RAF were in the Met Office at Northolt which is very close to Heathrow. One day an SAS airliner landed and when the pilot came into the Met Office he said, "Where is the passenger building?" And we replied, "Do you know where you are?" He then said, "This is Heathrow, isn't it?" He made what must have been an easy mistake by coming in on the wrong runway, just a short distance from where he should have been. Traffic then of course was nothing like what it is today.

My father, ready to take me to the recruitment centre,
on 27th July 1941, when I joined the RAF.

My parents sent me this photo when I was overseas.

In uniform, after a church parade.

Algerian scenes in 1943.

Roy Howe, the forecaster, and myself
outside the Met Office tent in Bo Rizzo, Western Sicily

In uniform at the YMCA in Catania.
The single ribbon is the Africa Star.

Jim Carlile and myself on the steps of Albergo Etnea, a rest camp
about 6000 feet above Catania on the slops of Mount Etna.

Tommy Hatton flies my model glider before he crashed it.

Jim Carlile's flying model of a Lysander aeroplane.

My model super fortress photo which came 1st in a magazine competition.

Geof Thorley, one of our wireless operators,
with the 'sparrow nut' which we rescued from torture by young children.

Golden Hind at anchor before leaving to go to Poole, Dorset.

Met Office and air traffic control building at Augusta, Eastern Sicily.

A flying boat commencing its take-off run.

Gathering speed before take-off.

On the Met Office roof.

The rest camp at Albergo Etnea.

Time off with the Varaschini family in 1945.
Left to right: Pat Varaschini, Major Wilson (Jimmy), Pat's father,
Pat's brother (Sonny), Mrs Varaschini,
Stan Gilman (another meteorologist) and me.

CHAPTER 4

Home at last

My first priority once I was back in civvy street, was to try and find a different job from Lloyd's Bank and I applied to Knight, Frank and Rutley, high-class estate agents in Hanover Square. I was offered a job in the Post Room which I accepted. The wages were so low (37s/6d) that I just could not afford to go to London, paying my own fare, and so with great reluctance I had to return to my previous employer and start work in the Sutton branch of Lloyd's bank just a short bike ride from home. One thing did amuse me when I was stuffing the letters for Knight, Frank and Rutley was to see an elegant sheet of notepaper addressed to the Dowager Duchess of… and the writer of the letter started it with 'Dear Flossie'.

Work in the bank was very tedious, sorting cheques and writing statements and once every fortnight was balance day when we often had to work very late. Life did become more tolerable when I was moved to the Banstead branch and became a cashier. I therefore had daily contact with the customers and as Banstead is more or less on the edge of the countryside there are more retired people living in the area. This meant that we cashed more cheques for people than the money we took in from traders, with the result that each week we had to order £2,000 in £1 notes, and £1,000 in 10/- notes from Head Office. These parcels were known as HVPs (High Value Packets) and had to be collected from the main Post Office. To do so from our branch the rule said two people must go together; one carrying the special bag with a chain to go round your wrist. That would have meant leaving Mr Clarke, the manager, alone in the bank as there were three of us in this small branch. Leaving him alone was also breaking a rule so we decided we'd have to break one of them and I would cycle to the Post Office and put the HVPs in my saddle bag. This I did throughout the two years I spent at Banstead so in total I brought back something like £300,000 in my cycle bag to the branch.

Mr Clarke was a delightful man to work for and a very popular manager because he was a scratch golfer and usually beat the General Managers when they had their annual match. When he retired I always called on him when I was visiting Devon and one day, when I was 70, he looked at me and said, "How old are you now?" and when I told him he said, "Serves you right!" – he was always ready for a joke and a laugh. Even when he had an accident in his Rover car he told me about it and said – "and it was a good one!"

At one stage when I was working in Banstead we had a very eccentric customer who was a retired school teacher. She lived about a mile away and drove a small pre-war Morris 8 saloon car. She didn't know how to change gear so drove everywhere in bottom gear. She always wore her black school gown over clothes that probably were hardly ever changed and wore a sort of hat that made her look like a witch. When she came in the bank she was very often carrying an enamel pail full of fishes' heads and scraps from the local fishmonger to take back to feed her animals. The smell from the fish remains and her clothing were so powerful that Mr Clarke always threw open all the windows even in mid-winter and then sprayed the bank hall with a FLIT-Spray. If she cashed a cheque it was usually for 10 shillings and she'd pass the grubby cheque book over to me to make it out for her, even asking me to sign it, saying – "I am such a duffer."

When she died, the bank had been made executor of her will so Mr Clarke and I had to go along to her bungalow to make the necessary arrangements for it to be sold. There, we got a huge shock when we got inside. She had been living in the kitchen with some of her animals – a goat had a pile of straw in one corner and two or three hens had another corner for their perch but when they stood on the handset of her telephone, their droppings had completely buried it. The council used to inspect the place at regular intervals because, of course, there were many rats which they tried to control and one of these inspectors told us that in her lounge there had been a tea set laid out for two people and it had been like that, untouched, for as long as he could remember, which was over 10 years. My theory is that this was laid out for some special visitor who perhaps never turned up and her disappointment was so great it affected her mind.

On another occasion an elderly spinster who looked after her father came in, in a state of great agitation, and asked Mr Clarke to go back with her to help lift her father up from the floor where he had got stuck after trying to do his daily exercises. He did go and all was well.

My music teacher, Grace Humphery,
with daughter Margaret (in the Auxiliary Territorial Service – ATS)
and son Brian.

Back garden at my cottage in Chipstead, Kent.

Grape vine at the back of the cottage.

Making good use of the narrow home-made dining table in the cottage.

The greenhouse in the garden of the house in Beeches Avenue,
which was built by myself.

The Hillman Minx convertible car outside my house (left-hand)
in Beeches Avenue.

The bay next to Isola Bella, Taormina
where we had many lunches at the Beach Café (left).

Tea with Pat in the garden of her Taormina villa.

CHAPTER 5

BBC

In spite of these unusual diversions I was trying all the time to find another job and the only place I could think of was the BBC. I had no professional qualifications and my thinking was that if I could get on to the BBC staff there would then be many different avenues I might follow without actually changing my employer. After receiving many rejections from applications I kept on making, I decided to go to Broadcasting House personally and say I'd not heard the result of my latest application which was an announcer's post. When I got there, they looked up the correspondence and said, "We sent you a rejection letter on…" to which I replied with as much conviction as I could master, "Oh, well, I never got it." They then said, "As you are here, we will give you a voice test." Anthony Craxton, who at some time had produced the Queen's Christmas Broadcast, listened in another room to me reading a news bulletin which included items about the 1948 Olympic Games. When I'd finished, he came and said to me, "We wouldn't have accepted you anyway because you have signs of a cockney accent, especially the way you accentuate the 'pic' of Olympic."

At that time I happened to have a BBC diary in which the names of heads of department and other important officials were listed, amongst whom was Stuart Hibberd, Chief Announcer. I decided to ring him up at his home address which in the phone directory. He spoke very sharply to me and said I should not trouble staff at their private address but should write to the appointment department – back to square one. This, I decided, was not going to get me anywhere so the next thing was to call on people personally. This I did one day when the bank closed earlier than usual and I cycled to Bromley and knocked on the door of one of the officials. A lady opened it with a surprised look on her face and I said, "I am sorry to call on you like this, because you don't know me but I've come to see if your husband can give me a job." Her expression changed immediately to one of relaxed interest and she said, "That's most interesting and I think you have come to the right place." The rest is history and I joined the BBC at the beginning of 1951 and both the lady and her husband became my friends for the rest of their lives.

In 1953 I was sent to work at Alexandra Palace, the home of the first regular television service in the world which started in November 1936. One of my jobs when I got there was to buy the cine film from Kodak and Ilford for the newsreel and documentary cameramen. One day I asked one of them, who was going to film something for the newsreel, where he was going and he said to film the first computerised flight simulator; so I said, "Can I come with you?" "Of course," he said. It was somewhere in East London and when we got there I was amazed to see it was housed in a large 4-wheel trailer like a caravan. While the filming was going on I walked down the centre of this trailer and at one stage I had to move to one side between banks of valves (over 1500 of them) to allow him to film down the gangway. When I looked at the news on television that night I could see two eyes peering at the camera between the layers of valves.

On another occasion the same cameraman was going to film the holiday crowds on the beaches around the south coast. He was going to do this from Croydon Aerodrome and I only live 3 miles from there so cycled to meet him there – it was a bank holiday – and we spent a very interesting couple of hours in a Dragon Rapide aeroplane between Frinton in Essex, all round the coast to Bognor in Sussex.

While I was doing this job a very young David Attenborough came into my office and asked me to order some 100-foot spools of Kodachrome 16mm 'B' winding for a film he was going to make in West Africa. This turned out to be the first of his extremely successful series of Zoo Quest programmes.

After about 2 years doing this work BOAC (British Overseas Airways Corporation) started a new service to Trinidad and, as was usual in those days, the inaugural flight was filled with journalists, travel writers and newsreel cameramen. The BBC was invited to send someone and I went as an assistant to George Rottner who was the senior newsreel cameraman. What a contrast this all was from my unhappy days in the bank, even though I was still on a low salary.

Going to Alexandra Palace every day took 2 hours in each direction so I was quite pleased when I got a move to the Lime Grove Studios in Shepherd's Bush. We had offices in some of the nearby Victorian terrace houses but a lot of the live programmes came from the large film studio. During this period the new Television Centre was taking shape just down the road.

In the meantime in 1956 I got a new job in the recently formed Television Transcription Unit which had been created to supply complete BBC television programmes on film to overseas customers. This came about due to the amazing feat of getting pictures of the Coronation in 1953 on to North American TV screens on the same evening of the same day as the Coronation. It was done like this: High Definition TV screens (coloured blue) were filmed in Alexandra Palace (known throughout the BBC as AP) and during the transmission of the service from Westminster Abbey and the procession, relays of motorcyclists rushed the film to the processing labs. There the film was developed to negative form only (no printing because on transmission in North America it could be electronically converted to positive). After a quick edit back at AP the film was loaded into a waiting helicopter on the green outside the building and flown to Heathrow where 4 Canberra bombers waited to take off in relays, being re-fuelled in flight as they crossed the Atlantic. Their destination was Montreal and from there the film was rushed to the nearest TV transmitter. Due to the time lag of 5 hours between the UK and North America this gave a slight advantage to the very tight schedule.

My increase in salary meant I could now afford to buy a new suit! In the early stages, this new job was based in Bush House, the home of External Services and broadcasts to many countries in over 30 foreign languages. This gave rise to the fact that the Bush

House canteen had the reputation of being the best of all BBC canteens because it catered for many different tastes and was open 24 hours a day.

At about this time I felt like giving myself a good holiday, and through an organisation called Summer Schools Abroad booked a 3-week holiday in Rome where we were housed in the university building.

The holiday was called 'Art and Architecture in Ancient Rome' and our leader for the whole course was a fascinating Italian lady called Professor Dompe who was very short and quite fat. Her English was very good but her pronunciation most unusual. For example, she would say, "The Erbar of Rome was Osstia" (the harbour of Rome was Ostia). We all liked her very much as she was an excellent guide when visiting the various sights.

During this holiday I teamed up with a girl who was at Birkbeck College in London and when the holiday was over, several of the people came to my house to exchange holiday photos. My mother could see how well this girl and I had got on and after they all left she said to me in angry tones, "Don't you ever ask that girl here again!" We hadn't got to any sort of 'boy and girlfriend' stage but my mother was going to prevent that at all costs. This is the key to the blight that clouded the rest of my life and this is the most difficult part of my story to relate.

I have never really tried to analyse why events turned out the way they did. I was well looked after at home, but severe shortage of money was by far the main problem for at least 10 years from the age of 24. At one stage my mother applied to the Stock Exchange Benevolent Fund and was generously granted £4 per week for as long as she needed it. Even so we had seven envelopes, one for each day of the week and every Sunday we put 7s/6d in each one for daily essentials like food, bread and milk. The rest of the money went on rent, rates, gas, water, electricity and fuel. If there were any coppers left over on Saturdays, we had a bar of chocolate. New clothes were out of the question, but of course, wartime rationing had more or less schooled us into this way of living anyway.

I suppose the constant restraints on my emotional development had a very strong effect on the subconscious – so much so that quite recently, almost 20 years after she died, I have had some very disturbing and unexpected dreams in which I am actually hating my mother. It's also very significant that when I think about it I never once put my arms around her to give her a long hug – nor did I ever call her by the friendly "Mum". It makes me feel very sad to write this, but the past cannot be changed.

It had occurred to me that perhaps there is a gene on my mother's side of my family that makes me similar to my Aunt Edie and Uncle Jim and Char because none of them ever got married. Aunt Edie hated my mother from the day she was born, 4 years after Edie, because she said so to her face. This unfortunately led to a long gap of nearly 20 years when there was no contact with either my aunt or uncles and my mother and myself, and it was only in 1966 when Aunt Edie rang my mother and abruptly said, "You'd better come and see your brother Char," who had a stroke which quickly led to his death. I had so missed the contact with them over those long years because I always felt great affection for all of them.

Although I had been terribly spoiled during my childhood, my mother's manner later became one of domination which perhaps I put up with far too much. I should have left home, of course, but that was impossible because of the money situation and my income, with all the struggles I'd had to get into the BBC, was so low.

On the whole, I was enjoying my time at the BBC and progress was improving. I joined the local tennis and badminton clubs near my home and made quite a few friends so that in 1957 I got together a party of 12 of us, 5 men and 7 ladies and made all the holiday arrangements myself to go as a group to Sicily where I knew a Danish lady who ran a most attractive pensione – Villa San Pietro – in Taormina. I had known Miss Mogensen during the war and because it was not wise to open the front door after dark, the people she knew always sang or whistled a theme from Tchaikovsky's ballet music before she opened the door. This holiday was a real success not only because we saved at least 30% over travel agent's costs, but also because we included weekends in Naples and Rome during the 17-day break.

During the war years, I had no access to a piano for anything like regular practice, so when I had settled down to a civilian life in the late 1940s I resumed piano lessons with my pre-war teacher. Although she'd thought I could be a concert pianist in the pre-war days, I knew I could never do that because before playing in public like music festivals, I suffered terribly from nerves and was even sick before starting any performance in public. However, at one stage I was persuaded to play a 2-piano duet with a girl I knew quite well and enter the Horsham Music Festival. Because I had the support of another person, I felt hardly any nervousness, with the result that we came first in our particular class.

I have maintained the ability to continue playing but not to the standard of years ago. One of the things I used to notice was that when I was asked to play something at any sort of gathering, all I knew were classic pieces and as soon as I started playing, the cheerful sound of party chatter would suddenly stop and for a while the party spirit was killed stone dead. To overcome this, I learnt a number of George Gershwin's well known tunes and one or two by Billy Mayerl which did the trick and kept the party going.

In 1960, I was quite surprised to be offered a general training course within the BBC to learn about every avenue included in the Corporation. Lectures were given by Heads of Departments such as copyright, legal affairs, accounts, central services (looking after buildings), catering as well as all the broadcasting departments such as music, drama, children's programmes, light entertainments, news etc, both in radio and television. It was all most interesting especially as I still nursed a secret desire to do something nearer the microphone. What was surprising was the fact that when a head of any department gave the lecture it was always to the point and well presented, but when anyone less than the head of the department had to stand in, the difference was most noticeable.

I cannot remember whether the course lasted 4 weeks or perhaps a bit longer but without a doubt I would, in later days, sometimes encounter a situation when I could say, "Well, when I was on the training course, they told us to do so and so." Soon after this, I moved to a new position in the unit supplying BBC recordings overseas and this involved travelling to the major BBC regions throughout the UK to find out what new projects were under way which might not necessarily be on the full TV network. Bristol in particular having formed the Natural History unit produced very sale-worthy programmes such as the long running 'Look' series with Peter Scott and our idea was to notify customers of forthcoming programmes which might be of interest to them.

Another rise in salary meant I could now afford to buy a second-hand car, but I was choosy about what the car should be. Firstly it had to be a convertible and must not be black and the price had to be somewhere in the £500 range; also it had to be no older than 2 years with a low mileage. I was prepared to wait for all these conditions to be met and one day a friend of mine who was a solicitor put me in touch with a reliable dealer. Over a period of some months, this dealer would ring me and if it wasn't exactly what I wanted, I'd turn it down, except on one occasion he rang and when he said the car was black and I said no, he then said, "Well I think you should come and look at this one." I went to Warren Street, where the dealers met, in my lunch hour, and there was the most handsome Hillman Minx convertible. Yes, it was black, but the folding hood was red as was the leather interior and the wheels, and along the side of the car was a very smart red and chromium stripe. It was love at first sight and I decided this was the car for me, and indeed it was, because I kept it for 44 years and it gave me wonderfully reliable service over 150,000 miles. When Princess Elizabeth married Prince Philip she went with him to Malta where he was based and they ran an early model of this car. According to the log book, my car had been owned by a prince with a foreign sounding name for its first 2 years.

When the dealer brought the car to my home one Sunday morning, he put it outside my garage which was at the bottom of my garden. I sat in it for some time, wondering how to drive it into the garage. This was because I had taken the driving test and passed it on a driving school car over 2 years earlier and never had any further practices in driving a car. Very gingerly, I engaged first gear and managed to move the car very slowly into the garage. How was I going to get enough practice to venture out on the main road? Fortunately, there was a very quiet residential road nearby, and every evening when most people were at supper or watching television, I drove up and down this road. This went on for quite a long time, about 2 or 3 weeks, until one day I decided I must throw myself in at the deep end and drive to work which was now at Television Centre. I had studied the A-Z London road map and worked out the route, but the most harassing part was going round the one-way system at Hammersmith Broadway. Having parked the car without further incident I almost felt confident that evening as I was driving home and wondered why I'd been so cautious for the first few weeks.

At about this time, I thought of a way to earn a bit of extra money. I would go round to various estate agents in the district and ask if they'd like me to provide photos of some of the houses they had for sale. This was long before the days of instant photos, in fact no photos ever appeared in office windows, just the written description. The idea was accepted by 3 or 4 agents and I was soon quite busy taking black and white photos, and developing, enlarging and printing them all for the sum of 5 shillings per photo (25p in today's money, but worth about £5 today).

On one occasion, the lady of the house asked why I was taking a photo of her house and when I explained, she said, "Would you take some pictures of my children?" I'd never done such a thing in the past, so I said I would try and we arranged for me to go there on the next weekend. The boy was about 6 and the girl 2 years younger. I started playing with them on the lawn with a ball so that they did not feel shy. Then I set up my camera on the tripod and set the camera on automatic time delay so that I could run round and continue the game with them. Perhaps I should not say this, but the result was spectacular and I charged her 5 shillings for each photo. They would both be in their late 50s by now.

As already mentioned, at about this time my job was taking me all over the country and I took a particular liking to the Scottish region where the headquarters were based in Glasgow, and with a little bit of persuading I managed to be sent there on a 6-month attachment to the Programme Planning Department in July 1964. This turned out to be one of the happiest periods during my 32 years with the BBC.

When I first got there, they gave me names and addresses of various places I could stay, but after looking at one or two of them, I did not like the areas. One day I said to my office colleagues, "If you had unlimited choice, where is the best place to live in the Glasgow area?" And with almost one voice, they said, "Oh, Bearsden or Milngavie – out at the western end of the city." So the next Saturday morning, I went to Bearsden and stopped people in the street asking them if they knew anywhere I could stay as a paying guest. Then one person said, "Well, Mrs Veitch out at Langfaulds Farm might have a vacancy." Off I went to this place and when a surprised lady opened the door, she said, "How did you know I take in paying guests, because I never advertise?" Luckily she had a spare room and I spent 6 glorious months there.

During the first few days after I moved in, I had great difficulty understanding the strong Glasgow accent. There were two daughters, 14 and 16 and the husband, 'Drewy', who very much enjoyed his whisky on visits to Stirling Market with his pals; they all made quite a noise when they all came back to the farmhouse in the evening. When they met me for the first time, one of them said, "Who's that?" Followed by, "Well now if you go out to my car, on the back seat, there is a salmon – go and fetch it in." When I got to the car, the only thing on the back seat was an unopened bottle of whisky, but I guessed that was what he wanted and of course, I had to have a drink out of it after he had told me to take out the cork and throw it away, because as he said, "we never put the corks back."

74

On my first morning at work in Glasgow, my new boss greeted me with the words, "We've got an unusual problem, I wonder if you can help us with it. A lady has recently died in Ayr and in her will she has left the BBC her piano in gratitude for all the hours of musical pleasure the radio has provided her with. We'll send you in a car to her house and I want you to go and look at this piano to see if you think we should accept it or not." When I got to the house, the first thing I noticed was a Boudoir grand piano in the lounge covered in dust with the lid closed over the keys. Very gingerly, I lifted the lid and there was the magic word 'Bluthner'. I was taught for many years on a Bluthner and know just how good they are and even in its present state there was no hiding the quality of the instrument.

When I got back to the office, I went straight to my boss and said, "Accept that piano and spend whatever it takes to bring it up to scratch, because it will be worth it." Some years later, there was a series of programmes from Glasgow called 'The White Heather Club' and in the background could be seen a white grand piano – that's the piano I rescued.

I shared a large office with two announcers and three other people and on one occasion, one of the three disappeared after lunch. Nothing was said but next morning each of us had a neat little parcel which contained a slice of fresh salmon.

When the Edinburgh Festival started, I was sent to the BBC offices in Edinburgh in order to look after two visiting TV cameramen from Czech TV who'd come to film various aspects of the festival. One day Mr Polak asked if I could arrange for them to film inside a whisky distillery. Fortunately I had at my disposal a car and a local driver, Peter Waugh, and he'd done many jobs for the directors of Bell's Whisky. He arranged for me to take the two cameramen to the directors' meeting room where we were greeted with a huge bottle of Bell's liqueur whisky in the middle of the table. Large measures were poured out for each of us and I had no idea how strong this stuff was. Consequently much of the meeting disappeared in a haze which seemed to cover the arrangements which were made without my help. Needless to say it was good publicity, because from that day on, I have always bought Bell's whisky whenever I've had the chance. Another benefit by way of Peter Waugh was taking home a box of 12 freshly smoked kippers from the Leith docks areas. I've never tasted anything quite like those kippers from that day to this.

The long light evenings were continuing at the time when I was staying with my RAF friend, Jim Carlile, and his family. We'd have an early supper then manage to get nearly a round of golf before it got too dark. The family had a dog called Prince which they had rescued from a dogs' home and this dog obviously had a bad experience involving Volkswagen cars because whenever we were out in Jim's car and his 9-year-old son John and Prince were in the front seat, if John recognised a Volkswagen coming the other way, he would have to quickly put his hand over the dog's eyes, otherwise the dog would go wild with barking and growling. He only ever did this with Volkswagen cars.

After 3 weeks this pleasant interlude came to an end and it was time for me to return to Glasgow. Jim wouldn't take any money for my stay with them, so I bought him a golf club and gave Betty, his wife, a crocodile handbag which seemed to please them both.

I had joined a walking club soon after arriving in Scotland and most weekends I went out all day either on Saturday or Sunday in all kinds of weather. One of my favourite areas was not very far away near a place called Drymen on the eastern side of Loch Lomond and at the right time of the year you could catch the marvellous sight of salmon leaping up into the spray of a fast flowing waterfall at a place called the Pots of Gartness. At times there might be 3 or 4 salmon in mid-air together. Every now and again, they would aim in the wrong direction and would land on the hard rock either side of the waterfall and after a great deal of wriggling would eventually flop back into the lower water to try again.

Back in Glasgow on a couple of occasions, I was invited to go with the Planning Team to London for a general Planning Meeting at Television Centre. On the first visit we got an early flight to Heathrow which arrived in time for us to be at the meeting by

11am. We then got a late afternoon flight to Glasgow on the same day. On the 2nd visit our travels were by overnight sleeper on the train but that interrupted 3 days instead of one. As I still had 4 more months to spend in Scotland, I decided to take a late holiday as the summer months had been quite busy. I wasn't sure if I was doing the right thing to book up and go on a cruise because 30 years earlier my parents took me on my first sea trip, and the only other sea trip was my journey overseas in a troopship in the RAF during 1942. That first voyage in 1934 had been in a passenger carrying cargo ship from The Pool of London, round the south coast to Liverpool. The ship belonged to Coast Lines and was called *S.S. Southern Coast.* It carried about 100 passengers and was very comfortable. We set off on a Saturday and got to Liverpool on the following Wednesday then back to London by train. I was 12 at the time and enjoyed the shore excursions when we called at Plymouth and Falmouth. On the Tuesday, we rounded Land's End and entered a very rough sea all the way up to Liverpool. I knew as soon as I woke up I was going to be seasick and when my mother persuaded me to have some parsley soup at lunch time, I only got back to my cabin just in time to save making a mess anywhere else. The strange thing was that as I climbed the gangway to leave the ship at Liverpool, I was feeling dreadful but as soon as my feet touched dry land I was as right as rain.

In the 1960s, British India converted 2 of their troopships into floating classrooms to take school children with their teachers on educational cruises. The *Dunera* and *Devonia* each carried many hundreds of children with their teachers and any spare accommodation was open to the general public, so this was what I chose to do. The cruise itself was from Genoa to Naples and Greece ending up in Venice. Travel from London to Genoa was by train as was the return journey from Venice back to London. There were very few single cabins and I shared mine with 2 young chaps from Blackpool who were bus conductors. I was able to tell them a lot about that part of the Mediterranean because really they were out of their depth and this sort of thing was rather beyond their experience. When we called at Naples and the excursion was

77

to Pompeii, when they got back to the cabin they had no idea where they had been and said, "Cor, what a dump and waste of time; that was nothing but tumbledown ruins and rubble everywhere. We're going somewhere better after lunch; it's called Pompeii!" On another occasion I told them about the Greek currency and they said, "Where do you get these Draculas from?" When the sea was rough, I looked out of the porthole and said, "It's quite rough today; white horses everywhere," and they said, "What are they doing right out here?" I had a lot of good natural laughs with them.

The cruise was a great success for me and during the next 4 years I went on three more of them. The children on board were so well behaved and they had their own part of the ship to themselves. Lectures and film shows were very good and passengers like myself had our own seats in the balcony. I happened to be on board *Uganda*, another of the schools' fleet, just before it was hurriedly converted into a hospital ship and sent to the Falklands in 1982.

When I got back to Scotland at the end of the 1964 cruise, I only had a matter of about 2 more weeks before I was due to return to my permanent job at TV Centre back in London. It had been a most enjoyable experience working with all my new Scottish friends and there's no doubt about it, working outside the London area there is a much more relaxed atmosphere than some of the frenzy that seems to come over London from time to time.

I asked Mrs Veitch at Langfaulds Farm if I could use her lounge to invite about 8 of my closest BBC colleagues to a farewell wine and cheese party and she readily agreed to this, and provided some of the produce for me. So there were the 6 of us in the Programme Planning Department, the temporary boss who sent me to look at the piano when I first arrived and the Head of Programmes Scotland. I don't think her lounge had ever been used in such a way at any time in the past.

My Hillman car had given wonderful service over the past 6 months taking 5 of us on long trips such as Campbeltown in the Mull of Kintyre and many places further north without any sign of trouble. So at the end of 1964, I said a rather sad farewell to the Veitch family and the farmhouse where I had lived so comfortably and happily, and set off for the long journey south making a leisurely trip of it and breaking the journey overnight roughly half way.

At about this time my mother's sister, Aunt Edie, made a surprise phone call to say, "Your brother's in hospital, you'd better come and see him." As mentioned earlier in this story, there had been a rift between the two families and this was the first contact in about 15 years. Uncle Char, my favourite uncle, had had a stroke and was now in a very weak state in Orpington Hospital. I took my mother to see him as soon as possible but we only went once because he died shortly afterwards. We then had no more contact with my aunt, not even when she went to hospital after a fall in 1972 and died. All very sad for me because I loved staying with them in my school days. Quite surprisingly in my aunt's will she left me 3 cottages; all of them occupied and all in very poor condition. I shall have more to say about them a bit later on but she had obviously had a soft spot for me and before going to her funeral, we went to the undertakers and saw her in her coffin. This was the first time I'd seen a dead person and when I touched her forehead, it surprised me when I felt how stone cold it was. It also surprised me how much younger she looked, lying there peacefully with her eyes closed.

After 6 months away from London, I felt the contrast between working mainly in the field of Radio in Scotland rather than Television in London and soon after my return there was an advertisement for a post in Radio in Broadcasting House; a place where I had always hoped I might one day have a job. Fortunately in 1966 I was selected for this post and moved from TV Centre to Portland Place. I'd never quite felt I had the right temperament to be amongst Television people with their 'pushy' rather forceful ways and moving into BH (as we always called it), the difference became even more obvious. My job was still connected with supplying material of various kinds to the general public which was connected with Radio rather than Television but this was very much restricted by copyright and contractual obligations. Because it was a new department there were a number of problems which had not been encountered before, so progress was rather difficult. One day I was called to the boss's office and he told me they were going to make 3 or 4 of us into LP Record Producers; the idea being to transfer complete radio programmes onto LP records for sale to the general public. At first I expressed some doubt about my technical knowledge in doing work of this kind, but the boss said we were all in a situation which had never existed before and so persuaded me "to give it a whirl". It was in fact the start of one of the most interesting phases during my time at the BBC but unfortunately it only lasted just on 4 years.

Many of the LPs produced during this period were of special interest such as the sound of trains and aeroplanes in action. One of my assignments was to take a mobile tape recorder down to the Dart Valley Railway at Buckfastleigh in Devon to make a sound recording of all the activities on the railway from the time the early morning staff got the first train ready for its trip, right throughout the day until everything was put away at the end of the day's proceedings. On another occasion I made a recording of the Veteran Car Run to Brighton which is held each year in November. These recordings were used to augment items that had been broadcast on the radio. A very successful Radio 3 series which was called 'Britain's Cathedrals and their Music' provided enough material for several LPs with John Betjeman as the narrator. Due to a slight technical problem, I had to visit him in his London flat to re-record a short section, which we did in his bedroom where it was quiet. At a certain point he had to introduce a piece of music, but at the very moment when he gave its title, a noisy dust cart pulled up outside his window and the recording, which I still have, goes like this: "Now we will hear a piece of music by Elgar called... There's that bloody dust cart!"

One of my colleagues at this time had been Manager of Radio Luxembourg in his early days when advertising on the radio was a rarity, but I didn't have the opportunity to meet many well-known people because, by the very nature of the work, they already existed in recorded form. After about 2 years in this job it became more and more apparent that I couldn't do anything right for the man in charge of the section and it was quite clear that we didn't like each other. As things got to a certain pitch I was eventually removed from the post and made redundant. All I can remember saying in my defence was that of all the LPs that had been produced, those that had been my responsibility outnumbered, in sales terms, most of those that my 3 colleagues had made.

On the day I was removed from the job of LP Record Producer, life presented one of its bleakest aspects to me and for some time I was at a loss as to how I should face up to the situation. Not only was I at the difficult age of 48 for being found alternative employment at around my current salary level, but I had thoroughly enjoyed the work that had now been taken away from me. Going home in the train that night, I tried to decide how to handle matters indoors and amongst my closest friends. Should I pretend that everything was going on quite normally, or should I say straight away to everyone exactly what had happened? I decided that to keep it dark would have produced too much bottled-up strain and sadness and would probably have made me ill, so when I began telling the truth to everyone, I was most surprised to find how supportive and helpful they all were. This was very comforting and although I was without a permanent job for nearly 2 years the attitude of all those around me kept my hopes and spirits alive.

In spite of all this turmoil going on I spotted a photograph in the *Daily Telegraph* of a flying boat (one of my passions in life) which had arrived in Southern Ireland. It was owned by Capt. Charles Blair who was married to Maureen O'Hara. She had a home there and Capt. Blair ran a small airline in the Virgin Islands called Antillies Airboats. He was on a private visit to this side of the Atlantic and I was desperate to get over to Ireland to see the flying boat and meet him, so I rang Dublin Directory Enquiries to ask if they had Maureen O'Hara's telephone number and they did! So I said, "Can you put me through please." Very soon a lady's voice said, "Hello," to which I said, "Is that Maureen O'Hara?"

and she said, "Yes." I was so surprised to have got through like this that I did not have a short conversation with her but simply said, "Can I speak to your husband please," and Capt. Blair came straight on the line. I briefly explained my interest in flying boats and of course my RAF connection with them by being a meteorologist on a flying boat base in Sicily during 1945/6. Then I said, "I'd love to come over to see your Sandringham flying boat," to which he said, "Come right over."

I spent 5 glorious days with him and his crew on Lough Derg, sharing a bottle of sherry each evening and on my last day there had been the supreme excitement of flying in it down the river Shannon and back.

That machine started life as a Sunderland during the Second World War when over 700 were built mainly for Coastal Command. When the war was nearly over a number of them were converted back to civilian use and this one spent some years in Australia and New Zealand before Capt. Blair bought it and thoroughly brought it back to flying condition.

When Capt. Blair visited Calshot on Southampton Water a short time after my visit to Ireland, he was giving short flights to the general public, so I joined the queue but all tickets were sold out. When Capt. Blair and his co-pilot W/Cdr. Gillies came past the queue to enter the plane he spotted me and I said, "All sold out," so he said, "You come with us; you can sit behind the cockpit!"

Sadly, Capt. Blair was killed in an accident, taking off in one of his airline planes in the Virgin Islands in 1978 and the Sandringham flying boat is now in the Southampton Aviation Museum.

Although I was now out of a job, I remained on the BBC payroll as a supernumerary and placed in temporary positions wherever they were short-staffed. As a result, I found myself back at Alexandra Palace which had become the headquarters of the newly created Open University. The work consisted of writing the linking announcements between the end of one programme and the beginning of the next one – BUT – they had to exactly fill 22 seconds without sounding too slow or too fast and this was sometimes quite tricky. On another occasion I was offered the job of Central Services Manager at Broadcasting House which meant being responsible for the cleanliness of all the public areas such as meeting rooms, the canteen and washrooms, but I turned this one down. I didn't want to end my days, even in my favourite location, of being the lavatory cleaner when I had had such high hopes in those far distant days in the past when I had dreamt of working there.

A few more months went by and the next time I was offered a permanent position it was made quite clear that if I didn't accept this one, I would have to resign from the BBC, so of course I took it. It was in the field of personnel work but the great advantage was that I couldn't have had a nicer new boss, so much so that we became friends and he and his wife visited my home. I took up the position in 1972 and although the grade of the post was lower than my previous one, I retained the higher salary on a personal level so life suddenly became much rosier again, especially as 6 years later when my boss retired I was chosen to take his place. This was on a level much higher than the post I'd been thrown out of. I was now known as Special Assistant to the Director of Personnel.

One of these special duties involved the recruitment of people for the Overseas Services, covering more than 30 different languages of the world. Candidates had to have up-to-date knowledge and possibly experience of life in the country of their particular language, and this often presented problems. However, I was now firmly based in 'BH' and after 4 more years reached retirement age in 1982.

During the 16 years that I worked in Broadcasting House I was often able to go into an empty studio during part of the lunch break and do some practice on a piano that was usually in there. This was very useful because for several years Dr Ian Smith and his whole family organised very successful charitable concerts in their own house and inevitably my contribution was on the piano and my mother played her popular tunes well into her 80s. Even though Dr Smith was my GP, our friendship started when his wife Mary was pushing their second daughter Caroline in her pushchair past our house and Mary got talking to my mother who was in the front garden. That was over 50 years ago.

Melanie, their eldest daughter, used to take charge of technical matters such as tape recording the entire proceedings. My most successful effort was to play a 2-piano duet with myself. On the day of the concert, I went to their house after breakfast in order to tape record the bass part of the 2-piano duet and then on the evening of the actual concert, Melanie stood by to start that bass recording when I gave her the signal and at that moment I started playing the treble part of the duet 'live' on the piano to produce the 2-piano effect. It worked pretty well yet strangely enough I found it quite difficult to keep exact time with my own recorded bass. The piece itself was quite lively and tricky, from the 'Scaramouche' suite by Milhaud. Each concert consisted of a wide range of performances from young and old – singing, violin solos, poetry readings, extracts from the stories of Dickens, guitars – Martin, who played his penny whistle when he was six, lived next door. No one ever seemed to want to go home at the end of these concerts. What a show it would be if only we could assemble extracts from the tape recordings which probably still exist.

Traditionally, BBC people at a certain level were offered retirement lunches and because of my close association with Bush House and the Overseas Services, the Controller of Administration there invited me to just such a lunch. However, my director had also planned a similar one for me as well, so I had two farewell lunches. These lunches at the time had to be delayed for almost a year because no suitable candidate could be found to take over on my actual retirement date. This was all to the good from my point of view because those extra months (8 in all) were added to the calculation in working out my pension.

Before reaching retirement another blow was about to fall on me when, in 1979 my mother suffered a stroke and spent some time in hospital. When she came home I was faced with a very difficult situation as this was in the days before there was a proper carers' organisation. I had to move a bed downstairs and fortunately she fairly soon was able to walk about. I then had to organise Meals on Wheels, visits to the Day Centre and also weekly hospital visits for bathing. This was all on top of my last 3 years of full-time working. When I did retire I needed some sort of break from this relentless caring way of life, so I decided to do a voluntary job of running the Red Cross Library at Banstead Mental Hospital on 3 days a week. This at least got me out of the house but by 1986, after 7 years of this very demanding lifestyle, I was on the verge of a breakdown. Fortunately my GP knew of a lady, only a mile away, who ran a very small residential home with only 5 residents. I said to my mother that I planned to visit my Vancouver cousins and happily she agreed to go to this place. When I came back and visited her she said, "I don't want to come home; it's so nice here." What a relief that was and I never had the guilty feeling of putting her there against her will. Having no brothers or sisters and no local relatives, every aspect of caring had fallen on my shoulders for the whole of those 7 years and until one experiences a situation like this no words can ever convey the extreme stress, fatigue and isolation that this creates.

BBC colleagues on a visit to my cottage.

The house at Langfaulds Farm, near Glasgow, where I lived for six months.

Mr and Mrs Veitch in the kitchen at Langfaulds Farm.

Countryside around the farm.

Jim Carlile and his son, John, on the banks of the Firth of Forth.

Jim and his wife, Betty, with my mother on a visit to the cottage.

CHAPTER 6

Retirement

If I look back over the entire working period of my life, starting with that first day in Lloyds Bank when I was 17 and ending with the last day at the Red Cross Library when the hospital closed and I was 64, I think I can say I'm reasonably happy with the way things turned out throughout those 47 years. Life always has its ups and downs and when I had a burning desire to be a meteorologist when I was 12, within 5 years I became one, albeit in the RAF which I could not have foreseen. Then when I dreamt of working in Broadcasting House, I eventually did so for 16 years until I retired at quite a respectable level.

I would far rather prefer to have become a family man instead of the solitary figure sometimes floundering through life alone (how I hate being in hotels and restaurants by myself), but now in 1986 with my mother happily cared for, life was about to change completely. The biggest change that occurred was the fact of living entirely alone – and I didn't like it.

In order to overcome this problem, I decided to take in student lodgers and got in touch with 'Hosts'. This did not provide a suitable answer but out of the blue a friend of mine in London told me he knew a Vietnamese family who ran a cheap jewellery stall in the Portobello Road Market and one of the sons, who was 24, acted as interpreter for his mother on the stall when he wasn't studying at the Hammersmith Further Education College for his GCSEs (at 24!). Because he had no quiet space for study at home he might be interested to stay with me. I said, "Bring him along to my house," and while he was here he said he would like to come and when I asked, "When?" he surprised me by saying, "Tomorrow." He was painfully shy at the start and also terribly afraid of the dark. If I was invited to friends in the evening I had to ask my cleaning lady, Olive, to come in and play cards with him till I got back. I grew fond of him because of his difficult background as a refugee but when I had to go into hospital for a hernia operation, he decided to go home but did not come back.

Soon after this a second lodger came along whom I got talking to in a library. His was a most interesting case because he was a lecturer at Tianjin University in China and the reason for his visit to the UK was to make arrangements for a party of professors to visit the East London Polytechnic (as it then was). Unfortunately, his visit coincided with the Tiananmen Square episode and his flight out of China to the UK was the last one to leave for some time and in these circumstances on arrival in the UK he was given Indefinite Leave to Remain. After his arrival in my home he approached the Guildhall School of Music & Drama for his wife to join a violin course there, so I had both of them staying with me. She was already a first class violinist and when they spotted an advertisement for an audition to set up a new orchestra for the brand new Concert Hall in Athens, they jumped at the idea. The audition was held in Edinburgh and the two main judges were the conductor of the new orchestra and the leader of the first violins. The set piece was Glazunov's Violin Concerto so I know every note of that piece backwards, forwards or sideways because I heard her practising it every day till they went to Edinburgh. Her hard work paid off though because when she finished playing at the audition, the two men jumped up on the stage and flung their arms around her, saying, "You must come back to Athens with us," which she did, leaving her studies at the Guildhall uncompleted.

So after only less than a year with me they both went to live in Greece where I visited them on 4 occasions, the last one being to see their twin girls who were by now a year old and made a terrible noise when I held them in my arms. When they were born, I sent them a short poem, which went like this:

> Now that you're a mum and dad
> Which makes you feel so very glad
> Who is this little thing?
> Oh, this one's Ting and this one's Ling

and that is exactly what they called them! (Doubling each name Tingting and Lingling.) They have turned out to be world class musicians themselves and are at present studying in Vienna; one on the violin and the other on the cello. There is a disappointing postscript to this story in that the marriage fell apart and after divorce the ex-husband is now in Canada but the twins still have a home with their mother in Athens and she is still a member of the same orchestra in that city.

I was beginning to enjoy these activities and in all I've had a total of 7 students over a period of 25 years. But the greatest benefit of all is due to the last 2, Ding and Moon, who have now become the substitute son and daughter I have never had. Ding came to my place from China in 2001 and married his childhood sweetheart, Moon, in 2007 after which she went to Surrey University. Ding had been to Keele and Royal Holloway universities. Both of them now have good jobs and live in their own flat just 10 minutes' walk from my house.

All this has filled a large part of my social life in the course of which I've met and made friends with quite a number of people from many walks of life. Quite a few of these friends had same-sex partners and I always felt like the odd man out when I was with them because I never had a close partner of either sex but enjoyed being with those that did. It was as though the absolute determination of my mother to keep me to herself had the effect of locking up any passionate desires I might have in a safe and throwing away the key. I think she was like this because in 1946 she had only just lost her husband and I was already in my mid-20s when I came out of the RAF and she probably thought I might soon get married and leave home, and she wanted to prevent that at all costs – and succeeded.

I am fortunate in having a wide range of interests from Music to Aviation and Science, to the Arts and Love of the Countryside, Walking and Travel and under each of these headings I've developed a number of hobbies. To this day I still have a Comprehensive Model Railway which is laid out in the attic and when Ding had been with me for about 2 years I was offered a

Hornby gauge O Schools' Class engine and tender. I had longed for one of these back in 1938 when they first came out but in those days we couldn't afford it (at £2 2shillings). Now its price was £1150 which I quite happily paid after waiting 75 years. Ding looked on in amazement because my desire to own this thing was completely beyond his understanding and his remarks were, "Why does a grown man want to own something that was made for children 75 years ago?"

When I got to know more about astronomy I decided to make my own sundial and as can be seen in the pictures, the various rays of lines represent one hour for the shadow from the gnomon to run along one line and then an hour later down the line next to it – and each angle between the lines is different from the one next to it, and I got them all dead right. I once had the great honour of being invited to Sir Patrick Moore's home, mainly to see his garden observatory, but it poured with rain which meant we had a wonderful conversation instead.

Due to my interest in Preserved Steam Train Railways, part of my job in the late 1960s was to visit the Dart Valley Railway which ran from Buckfastleigh to Totnes in Devon in order to record all the sounds of that railway within one day. As I was settling down in a field waiting for the last train of the day to return to Buckfastleigh, I began to feel something crawling up my leg, but I dare not move because the recording microphone was switched on and any movement would have spoilt the sound of the passing train. It was very uncomfortable because I was sitting on an ants' nest but the recording was a success and I was able to deal with the ants afterwards.

Although the British Broadcasting Company began transmissions in 1922, the British Broadcasting Corporation came into being in 1924 and my father must have been one of the first people to buy a wireless set because in his cash book, which I have still got, there is an item in 1925 for '£10 Wireless Set' and I've also still got that in working order even if it is a crystal set.

On one of the visits to my cousins in Vancouver I made a trip on The Royal Hudson Train, which is now a tourist attraction. It runs on certain days north from Vancouver about 30 miles up the west coast of British Columbia to Squamish and it is the actual Royal Train used for George VI and Queen Elizabeth during their Royal Tour of Canada, in 1939.

In years gone by I've tried to grow exhibition sweet peas but with not much success and of course many hours were spent at my grand piano trying to improve Chopin and Rachmaninoff studies or Beethoven Sonatas with perhaps a bit more success. Maybe my lack of success in the line of horticulture was because although I built my own greenhouse just after the war it was with ill-gotten materials that I brought home bit by bit on my bicycle from the remains of a bombed-out-house, and this greenhouse was never any good in nursing delicate young plants into sturdy exhibition winners. I went to great lengths getting manure from the nearby smallholdings, cycling there pulling a wooden orange box fixed to the 4 wheels of my own original pram. One night I was loading this box with pig manure but had not realised just how heavy it was. As I struggled to tow it behind my bicycle up a hill, when I got to the top I sat back on the saddle to take a bit of a rest as we free-wheeled down the other side. Suddenly I was shocked to notice the pram wheels with the heavy box on board was overtaking me on the downward slope and in order to regain control I had to pedal hard to get in front of it again, with sparks coming off the iron rims of the wheels on the road as I tightened the towing rope. Luckily it was very dark with no traffic and eventually I got the load safely home, but got nowhere in the Sweet Pea Competition.

Throughout all these years, I've enjoyed tennis, badminton, golf and walking with rambling clubs. Most weekends would involve an all-day 10-mile walk, summer and winter, and as a result of these activities I have been blessed with a wide range of friends, some of whom I've known for many years.

My walking holidays nearly always took place at Whitsun each year round the Cornish peninsula from a base in Penzance. The cliff-top footpaths at that time of year are a riot of colour from the wild flowers.

When I shared an office with a lady who went somewhere different every year with her husband she once said to me, "Why do you go to the same place every year?" In reply I said, "Of the 10 years I've known you, all your holidays have been to different places and some not quite as good as others. In my case all my holidays have been a great success because I knew what I was going to get."

When I was on the committee of my walking club, I put forward a suggestion that we should get up and meet near the South Downs at 5.00am in order to see the sunrise from the top of the Downs at 6.02am. The chairman, a very lively 80-year-old who still led 10 mile walks said, "Well it's an unusual idea but we'll put it in the forthcoming programme, but I don't expect anyone will join you at that early hour." Much to everyone's surprise, including my own, 15 people arrived dead on time and we all went to a spot near Storrington on top of the South Downs and had a magnificent view of the sunrise at 6.02am after which we had breakfast from the boot of my car. From then on it became a regular feature in the club calendar until the years caught up on me and I couldn't do it any more.

Back in the 1950s soon after I joined the BBC, I've already mentioned how I gathered 11 friends together and with myself we organised a most successful holiday in Sicily. As a result of that trip, I got another 9 friends together from the Rambling Club and did virtually the same trip all over again just 18 years after the first one. Again it was a roaring success. I think the reason we all enjoyed both holidays so much was because after spending 3 years in Sicily during the war years, I knew the island so well and could take them to all the most interesting places. Lots of people are quite unaware how large Sicily is. It's the largest island in the whole of the Mediterranean and to go from one side of the island to the other is like going from London to Plymouth. I myself have been back 7 or 8 times since the war and in the year 2000 stayed with my old Italian friend in her villa at Taormina. She now has granddaughters and when I first met her in 1944 she was 17. Back in those wartime days she once told me a story I found hard to believe. Their large villa was open house to many different kinds of military personnel and she told me that an American fighter pilot had taken her to Catania airport where his single-seater fighter plane was based and sitting her on his knees had flown up to Taormina and back. When I stayed with her in 2000 I reminded her of the story and said, "That wasn't true was it?" To which she replied, "Oh yes, it was quite true!"

In 1960 six of us with 2 cars did a 2-week tour of Scotland, and this was before I had a car of my own or had not yet spent those 6 months working in Glasgow. In general terms we intended to drive north up the eastern side of England, tour across Scotland and come home down the western side. Peter and I were in his car with most of the luggage and Valerie and the other 3 girls were in her car. There was one snag. Peter always preferred to book our next overnight B&B in advance which meant we didn't know what sort of surroundings it would have. I on the other hand suggested we started keeping our eyes open from about 4.00pm onwards and when some place looked attractive we'd try and get fixed up there, but the drawback in this case was we sometimes had to stop 2 or 3 times before we found a vacancy for all 6 of us. We took it in turns to use Peter's idea one day and mine the next.

Near Balmoral we found a very nice place to stay which overlooked the Queen's Scottish home. We asked the owner to recommend somewhere for our evening meal and she suggested the Invercauld Arms Hotel which wasn't far away. It was a delightful place and during the excellent meal, Mary, who was quite a humorist, opened her handbag and took out her mascot penguin, held it over the table, waving it about and saying to it, "Have a quick look round!" and popping it back in her bag. On our way out I thanked the receptionist for such a pleasant visit and she said, "Well, you see, we have to keep up a high standard because we sometimes take the overflow from Balmoral."

Soon after this Scottish holiday I arranged to go to Italy with Summer Schools Abroad and we were housed in the buildings of Naples University. Much of the course was devoted to the famous eruption of Vesuvius in AD79 which devastated Pompeii and

Herculaneum. On one of the free days, a group of 4 of us went to Capri and when we got back to Naples it was quite late and we wanted a meal. In order to get back to the university we had to walk through what would be the open air street market in daytime. There we found a genuine trattoria with a wood-fire oven in the corner which was still open. While we were waiting for the pizzas, one of the lads in our group, who was a very good artist, made a sketch of the large Neapolitan who was doing the cooking. When he brought the meal to our table, the sketch was finished and he said, "Is that me?" and in reply the artist said, "You can have it." He was so pleased with it and said, "Grazie molto – no charge!"

Wending our way through the quiet narrow streets we came upon an unusual – but traditional sight. The dead body of an old lady was lying on a table at the front entrance to one of a row of houses and all the members of the family were sitting round this table talking very quietly (not easy for Italians) amongst themselves. This was around 11.00pm but I don't know how long they would sit there – well into the night I think.

I took a fancy to a little picture painted by a local artist of a very colourful view of the Bay of Naples with Vesuvius in the background. I kept enough liras in my wallet till the end of the holiday and intended to buy it on the last day of the holiday. It was on display in the market area and on my way to buy it, as I walked through the area, a lady on a third floor balcony was lowering her shopping basket to a friend in the street and as she did so two small boys ran towards me pointing this out and jostling me in the process. When I got to the stall with the picture, I put my hand in the pocket where I'd got the 5,000 lire note only to find it was no longer there. These youngsters had cleverly distracted me while one of them did the pickpocketing very expertly.

The Taj Mahal, Agra.

Japanese monks at the Taj Mahal.

My first student lodger, who was a 24-year-old Vietnamese refugee.

My final lodger, Ding, on graduation day at Keele University.

Ding and Moon on their Wedding Day.

The Sydney Opera House.

Japanese tourists in the rain at Kagoshima.

CHAPTER 7

New Interests

When my mother had been fixed-up permanently in the pleasant little residential home, I decided to go on a long cruise by flying to Hong Kong and joining the *Canberra* and sailing all the way back to Southampton via the Suez Canal, which was the major objective for me. An early part of this journey involved a visit to Bangkok where I was so impressed with the beauty of the many Buddhist temples. When I got home and showed my photos of them, one of my friends said, "You don't have to go all the way to Thailand to see Thai temples; there's a very good one in Wimbledon." I'd never heard of it before so made a point of finding it.

When I got there – yes it was just as beautiful as the ones I'd already seen but what impressed me just as much was the wonderful air of peace and tranquillity all over the grounds in which it stood. There was a lake and in the background was the elegant house in which the resident monks lived and this is what I photographed. It turned out pretty well so I had it enlarged and framed and took it to the temple where I saw the Head Monk and presented him with this framed photo. In reply he thanked me and invited me to stay to lunch. Monks always eat on their own before twelve noon so I had my lunch after that. When lunch was over I had a chance to meet several of the other monks, one of whom was called Mahalaow (that is how I shall refer to him but his official title then was Phramaha Laow Panyasiri). He came up to me and in very limited English said, "I like the way you speak – you teach me to speak English."

That was 25 years ago and since then I have been involved in a lot of his activities especially since he became Abbot of his own temple near Lichfield and now speaks fluent English but sometimes with amusing mistakes which he is quite ready to laugh at himself. It's during these 25 years that I have become increasingly attracted to Buddhism although I've made no positive moves to become a Buddhist. Throughout my life my parents weren't regular churchgoers and it was only when I joined the RAF and was asked what religion I belonged to that I had to really give some thought to being C of E (Church of England) and that is what my permanent identity discs which I wore had on them.

Back in the mid 1960s when I moved into Broadcasting House, I shared an office with a very pleasant young chap who was one of those very ardent Christians. Whenever we had a gap in our work he would get at me and say, "You ought to go to church – it would make life much happier for you." He persuaded me to go to the weekly Christian Union meetings held in the lunch hour and when he asked me to supper with his girlfriend I said, "That's very kind of you, but no thanks because that would mean the two of you could get at me."

I must say he had great faith in his own belief because when the troubles in Uganda were at their height he resigned from the BBC in order to go there as a Christian Missionary. When I pointed out to him what great dangers he would face, his reply was simply that Jesus would look after him. He did return after matters calmed down, completely safe, so I salute him for his faith. What he did to me though was to turn what little belief I had into a much stronger feeling that there cannot be an all powerful being 'who so loved the world' because there is so much strife and cruelty throughout all the races.

This then was the state of my mind when I first got involved with the temple in Wimbledon, and getting to know Mahalaow in the succeeding years showed me a much more acceptable way of life.

I do have my own ideas about what happens after we die. I don't think we just go out like a candle flame because I've had too many instances of unexplained happenings and the spirit or soul of a person is a real fact in my ideas and this is so difficult to define. It is certainly not finite in any way. The main reason I've given up C of E beliefs is because in church when we say the creed – it begins, "I believe in... etc." But I don't and therefore I would be a hypocrite if I still went to church and said those things.

When Mahalaow had become quite good at English he was made Abbot of his own temple in Birmingham. The building itself was an ordinary large residential place in the Aston area and I used to go there when he was studying at Birmingham University on a part-time basis to help him with essay writing. Apart from the fact that the subject matter was Buddhist-related, his written English was so disjointed and peculiarly phrased that I had to say to him, "Tell me what you are trying to say in this paragraph in your own words that I can understand." It was a very laborious process leading to an MA degree after which over a period of 9 years he gained a PhD which was quite an achievement considering it was for him gained in a foreign language. In the middle of that time he asked if I'd take him away for a few days so that he could have some peace and quiet for study away from the daily affairs of the temple. I booked up to stay at a furnished bungalow in Bembridge on the Isle of Wight. By a strange coincidence it was only a few yards away from the home of Rosemary Newbald that I used to go to school with when I was 6 – mentioned at the beginning of my story.

When I took Mahalaow to Osborne House we set off early so that he could have his lunch before twelve noon, but the café at Osborne House did not open till then and he was quite ready to go without lunch. I then pointed out that our clocks had been put forward one hour a few weeks earlier so that in reality, according to the position of the sun, twelve o'clock would really only be 11am GMT. So we both had lunch together. On the way back to our bungalow I found a completely deserted sandy beach which was lovely to walk on but the experience for Mahalaow was so intoxicating he ran along the sands as fast as he could with his arms outstretched and his colourful robes billowing out like wings – a sight very few must have ever seen but captured on my camera.

Later on I took him to my favourite part of the country in Devon. At one place where we stayed for Bed & Breakfast, we had a large room with 2 single beds and his was on the far side of the room from mine. Soon after I put the lights out he said, "My bed is cracking." So I went over to see if it was safe but what he had meant to say was, "My bed is creaking." We had tea-making facilities in the bedroom and when he saw the kettle he said, "Is that kettle for electricsity?" Which of course sounded funny to me. On the way home we called at Bosham by Chichester harbour and as the tide was coming in fast he said, "Is that water soda water?" Meaning of course, "Is it salt water?" So life on our trips together was full of fun and laughter.

A very strange incident happened when Mahalaow was at the temple in Birmingham. I had gone there to help with the preparations for one of their regular festivals and in the garden there were going to be a number of stalls and tables and chairs. One of the other helpers there was a Thai lady with her 2 sons; one was about 8 and Stephen who was about 6. Many people were staying overnight and these 2 boys were staying with their mother sleeping on the floor of the library which was on the ground floor. I was sleeping in a sort of attic up on the 2nd floor and the only window was a skylight set into the sloping roof. There was just room to get a single bed with the foot of the bed facing the entrance door and to get to it you had to go through Mahalaow's bedroom. We were all working quite late and I went to bed around 11pm. When Mahalaow came into his room he locked the entrance door as there were quite a few helpers also staying overnight that had not been there before. When I got into bed, it was pitch dark so I was soon fast asleep. At around 2 or 3am I was woken up by the sound of Stephen's laughter – I knew it was him because I'd kicked a football with him when we were in the garden. There was then the sound of someone like his mother going, "shh, shh" followed by more laughter. Then all of a sudden the bedclothes on my bed were pulled half-way on to the floor from the foot of the bed followed by complete silence. I then went back to sleep thinking that Stephen had crept upstairs to play this trick on me – not realising in my sleepy state that the outer door had been locked.

At breakfast next morning I related this story to his mother to which she replied, "How could he do such a thing as he was sleeping right beside me all night in the library?" When I told Mahalaow about it, his remark was, "You are not the first person to experience strange things happening in that attic."

The Birmingham Temple had one major problem. Whenever there were any special activities or festivals there was nowhere near the temple for visitors to park their cars because all the roads in the area were full of parked cars belonging to the local residents. For some months Mahalaow spent a lot of time and thought trying to find a suitable building and location. He has always been ready to suggest new ideas and sometimes has surprised me with his persistence in carrying out what I had thought at the time were a little beyond any possibility. I once said to him, "If you had been a businessman you would have been very successful."

Eventually a very attractive manor house came on the market at Kings Bromley, about 20 miles from Birmingham in the direction of Lichfield. It was situated in rural surroundings and had plenty of its own land surrounding the house; ideal for festivals etc. There was one snag – money; but this is where Mahalaow's abilities showed up most of all. He managed to secure a huge mortgage in spite of the fact that he himself had no capital nor did he have any regular income. I've often wondered how he did it. Once the move took place from Birmingham the atmosphere of the new temple was such a big improvement with delightful surroundings.

I mentioned earlier about the 3 cottages Aunt Edie had left me in her will. One of them was built by my grandfather (Wisdom not Priest) in the 1890s and my mother who was very young at the time laid the first brick. The other 2 were much older, probably before 1837, and each were '2 up and 2 down' with no indoor sanitation and one cold water tap downstairs over a stone sink – all very primitive. An elderly lady lived alone in each one so the first thing I did when I became the landlord was to investigate how to get a grant for a bathroom to be fitted in each one.

When I visited one of the ladies she showed me several marks at the side of the front room mantelpiece which gave the level of flood water whenever the nearby River Darenth had overflowed into her lounge, some nearly 3ft deep. My aunt had not been a very good landlord and both cottages were in a very poor state, so much so that when the council inspector came to see them in reply to my application for a grant, he immediately condemned both of them for human habitation and arranged for both tenants to be re-housed, which at first came as a shock to me.

Later, I realised I was now the owner of 2 empty freehold properties, which I was not allowed to use. I had a discussion with the estate agent who had been helping me and asked him what I should do and he said I could do one of two things – either sell them both as they are or keep both of them and employ an architect to turn them into one attractive modernised property. Selling both would have been at a very low price in view of the condition they were in so I decided to sell the 3rd cottage to the sitting tenant and, together with a bank loan, set about turning these 2 into my ideal country cottage. I was recommended to an excellent builder whose builder's yard was right next to the house where I was born; and he in turn put me in touch with a very good architect. All this took a great deal of time and effort especially as I was working full-time in London throughout the whole period. Very often I would say to my boss (the good one), "Do you mind if I have a long lunch hour today?" – then get a train to Sevenoaks where I'd be met and taken to where the work was being done, deal with what was necessary, back to Sevenoaks station to return to my office around 3.00pm. This sort of thing went on for about 3 years until one day in 1981 the builder rang and said, "Your cottage is ready for you to move in and the central heating is already working." I was delighted with what I saw on my first visit – with absolutely NOTHING in a brand new house interior – not even a teaspoon. This was going to be some task furnishing it the way I had in mind and I did have some quite definite ideas which I hoped to carry out.

Above all else I wanted to ensure the interior furniture and fittings were in keeping with a building that was probably more than 150 years old so I made a decision that the majority of the furniture would be good quality second-hand and by a stroke of luck a magnificent Ritmüller Boudoir grand piano was advertised in the BBC staff magazine just at this time, so this was my first purchase and of course it was the centrepiece of my 24ft through lounge. Because I was mainly interested in second-hand things I suddenly found many friends who were ready to give me all kinds of things such as dining room chairs, two pre-war armchairs (just right) and a full dinner service and tea set. This went on over a period of several years so that I found myself telling people how many different items had a story about them and how they came into my possession. The one major item I bought new was a high-quality fitted Axminster carpet throughout the lounge, dining room and stairs. It was called the Buckingham pattern and I was told it was used in Buckingham Palace. Upstairs I bought dressing tables with attractive walnut veneer and angle side mirrors with bevelled glass – from about the 1930s and one was £2.10p and another £4.00 because they were in a yard waiting to be taken away and destroyed. I also bought a Hoover with all its 1930s accessories in perfect order for 50p – just what I wanted.

Fortunately for me, the risk of flooding from the River Darenth had been almost eliminated because the last time this happened was in 1968. In that year there was a torrential fall of rain which flooded the whole street and as a result of this a very extensive flood defence system was built. It took the form of a very wide deep canal which started higher up the river and continued under the road straight into Chipstead Lake, which was in fact a deep gravel pit which had been allowed to fill gradually from the river and was now the home of the Chipstead Sailing Club. I tried to join this club but found that I was no sailing enthusiast – in fact I found it boring. The lake did, however, add greatly to the attractiveness of the whole area and my cottage was one of only 6 or 7 dwellings that had an unrestricted view across the green towards the lake.

I did not retire completely until 1986 when the hospital where I ran the Red Cross Library closed and my mother moved into the small residential home. I never had any plans to move from Carshalton to live permanently in the Chipstead cottage because I realised that many of my friends and important roots were in the Carshalton area and it is never very easy to build up these things when you are getting old in a new area.

I always remember one of my visitors saying, "We come into a country cottage and find a thoroughly modern kitchen downstairs and an equally modern bathroom upstairs, yet when we visit your Carshalton home, nothing has been modernised since 1907 when it was built." Yes that's quite true and I've even got the sealed-off gas light fittings which were in use when the house was first occupied. I do have central heating that was installed in 1985 but the scullery has the original tiled flooring and walls, plus a modern fridge and gas cooker. My paternal grandfather built the house and 4 of his 7 sons acted as his full building team. No wonder he became wealthy.

This is the house we moved to from Bessels Green in 1924 which we lived in rent-free till my father died in 1945. At that stage it was owned by his mother who had inherited many such houses built by her husband who died in 1925 so although she was a very wealthy lady, she was always very generous to the 5 of her children who all lived within the same area close to her home in Carshalton.

The Beeches Avenue in Carshalton is quite an historic road because it leads to the Oaks Park in which Lord Derby lived and the 2 famous horse races on Epsom Downs, the Derby and the Oaks, both owe their existence to gatherings that took place with Lord Derby in his country mansion there during the late 1700s. The River Wandle flows through Carshalton on its way to the River Thames and even today certain stretches of the river still grow wild watercress and in Anglo-Saxon times that fact was reflected in the name they gave to the area. I have always been glad to live in a district which is within walking distance of the open countryside with farms and small holdings and the Oaks Park is in that neighbourhood.

By inheriting a country cottage in Kent I was able to get the best of both worlds because my permanent home was within easy reach of London and the cottage, which was only 18 miles away, was in Kent, known as the Garden of England. It only took just over half an hour to get there by car so I gradually developed the habit of going there on a Friday evening and back on Sunday, ready to go to work on the following morning. The only trouble with such a routine as this is that you don't develop any 'roots' in the place because you are not there long enough and it's rather disappointing to me to realise that when I sold the place after 30 years, I did not leave behind any real friends. I had done most of my entertaining at the cottage because all the friends who came there were mostly from the London area. The usual remark that nearly all of them made when they first arrived was, "This place has such a lovely welcoming, warm atmosphere as soon as you enter inside." My interpretation of that, which I also always felt, was that Auntie Edie loved me to go and stay with her at the family home and so the gift of the cottage came with the spirit of her love for me throughout her life.

I mentioned the entertaining I did there and I made a specially narrow dining table for this purpose. As you entered the front door from the small outside porch you came straight into the first downstairs room. It had a lovely open fireplace which meant the table and chairs could not be placed too near the fire when it was (often) alight which is why it had to be narrow. I managed to get hold of a couple of tall wardrobe doors, 1930s style with walnut veneered wood, and fixed legs on both of them. At a pinch I could comfortably seat 8 people round this table but there was no room for large dishes with joints of meat waiting to be carved. That could take place on the other 'door' which was against the wall opposite the fireplace.

The main lounge had been the front and back rooms of the next-door cottage but the dividing wall and staircase had both been removed to provide a 24ft through lounge from the front of the house to the back and in this large space the 5ft 9ins grand piano fitted without any problems at all.

This piano was the very first item to enter the house before any carpets or furniture arrived and it so happened that when it was being unloaded, a near neighbour saw it go into the house. The next weekend when I was at the place, there was a tap at the front door and it was the person who had watched the arrival of the piano. His name was Eddy Banfield and he said, "As soon as I saw that piano being delivered, I had to know who owned it." Well of course we became great friends and he was a magnificent pianist of the 1930s Dance Band era. He very much admired Carroll Gibbons and his band at the Savoy, and Eddy himself had his own Dance Band in 1932 and broadcast at the BBC. Whenever I arrived at weekends he would often call and say, "Can I come in and play your piano for a little while?" I had 2 particularly musical friends from Carshalton and whenever they came to the cottage Eddy had to be brought in for some wonderful evenings of light music. Unfortunately Eddy had a heart condition and after only 18 months of this happy relationship, poor Eddy died.

The back garden presented quite a problem in those early days as the whole area was in the flood plain from the River Darenth; the soil was immensely rich, so much so that I used to tell people that when I planted peas, they would all get eaten up by slugs and snails but the twigs I'd put in to support them started to grow anyway. One weekend when I was visiting the cottage with my mother, the lady who lived round the corner in my mother's old home, happened to be passing by and said to her, "Would you like to come round and see what we've done to your old family home?" So next day we were both invited to tea and shown what a marvellous place they'd made with 3 bathrooms, a games room and swimming pool in the garden. We both could hardly recognise the old place we knew so well. Then she said how much the family loved it but there was one thing troubling them and that was their young son, about 5 years old, who kept waking up with bad nightmares shouting, "Don't let her come near me, she hasn't got a face." At this point my mother said, "Oh, I can explain what that

110

is all about" and went on to describe how her little sister, when she was 5 in 1899, went to a cupboard, "in this room over there but it's not there any more" to get a candle to take upstairs to bed, but when she held the lighted candle too close to her nightdress it flared up and burnt her face so badly that she died in hospital. The boy's mother then said, "Did you say the cupboard used to be over there?" (pointing) to which my mother said, "Yes, in the corner." "Well that is so extraordinary," she said, "because when we were looking over this house before we bought it, another couple were doing the same thing and when the lady stood near the spot you've just pointed to she shuddered and said – "Oh I couldn't live here, this house is haunted." Throughout this conversation the boy wasn't even in the house, he was out to play.

The happy end to this story is that when we again met the boy's mother a week or two later she said, "Mrs Priest – I'm so glad that you explained the story of your little sister because my son hasn't had another nightmare since then."

Whilst on the subject of strange happenings, I was in my cottage alone for the weekend when I went to bed and as I took off my vest, the label from the back of the collar fluttered to the floor – or so I thought. When I picked it up it wasn't a label from the garment at all; it was one of those address labels you can have printed to stick on the back of an envelope to show the sender's address and this one was of my RAF friend's address, and he had already died several years earlier. What is so strange about this is that we were such close friends we never had the need to write to each other so I had never seen this particular type of label ever before. When I explained this to a spiritualist friend of mine she wasn't in the least bit surprised and said, "Oh, that's an apport and it's simply to let you know you're in his thoughts."

One of my own beliefs is that coincidence is much more than just that. They happen so frequently to me and are always so strangely apt. For example, I was with a friend visiting Rochester where Short Bros built flying boats like the RAF Sunderlands which were used in the Second World War. I was particularly interested to see where they might have been built and tested on the river Medway because my year as a meteorologist on a flying boat base in Sicily was probably the happiest year of my life (1945/6). As we walked along the path beside the river in the shadow of Rochester Castle, I remember saying, "They must have tested them this side of the road bridge because on the other side there's no room for a take-off run." About 2 or 3 weeks after this I had a birthday and my doctor's family, who have been close friends for many years, sent me a birthday card as always. They had known of my close association with flying boats during my time in the RAF but what they didn't know was anything at all to do with my visit to Rochester a few weeks earlier. When I looked at the card I was astounded to see the castle at Rochester behind the footpath with an RAF Sunderland anchored exactly where I'd suggested they would have to be. The scene couldn't have been more like I'd imagined it if a photograph could have been possible. Coincidence? – No! Much more than that, to do with influences and forces about which we can have no knowledge nor proof of their existence. It may only happen to certain people, not everyone, rather like tuning in to a particular radio station which some people cannot get.

This leads me to the peculiar feeling I always get when I try to understand the mystery of time and space, both of which have no obvious beginning or end. The Big Bang Theory for the origin of the universe has the obvious flaw of not being able to describe what led up to it. For my part I try to think of all time as being NOW. If we think of TOMORROW, that will become NOW when it becomes TODAY and likewise YESTERDAY was NOW the day before. In other words, YESTERDAY, TODAY and TOMORROW have ALL been NOW at certain stages of their existence and so the whole of TIME is simply NOW. Space presents a different problem which I believe needs a radical re-think of what it is, because if you take an object like a ruler which is 12 inches long and divide it up into pieces an infinite number of times, by definition those pieces should stretch from the beginning of the ruler to infinity – but they don't, they only fill the space up to 12 inches; in other words there is a flaw in the way we think of that space of 12 inches and I'm not clever enough to even begin to think what that flaw is.

In chapter 1 I briefly mentioned the fact that I became a guide at the Croydon Airport Museum. I had been a member of the Croydon Airport Society for many years prior to this and it wasn't until 2006 that I was approached and asked if I would like to join the small group of volunteers as one of the guides. It has never occurred to me that I might be able to do such a thing but the fact that I had such a good memory of actual experiences way back into the distant past was the main reason for joining them.

The museum is open to the public, free of charge, on the first Sunday of every month between 11am and 4pm and on my first day I accompanied one of the regulars to learn the ropes. Next time, I was on my own, feeling rather nervous, but when it became apparent that my small group of visitors were showing signs of interest, I soon gained more confidence. Now, after 8 years' experience I have learnt a few tricks of the trade and I nearly always enjoy a full day at the museum once a month. I must be one of the very few people still alive that can actually talk about the experience of my 1938 trip to Paris with my father in the luxury of a 'Hannibal' class HP 42 airliner, in chapter 2. The 6 photos of airliners at Croydon Airport at the end of chapter 8 were taken by me in 1939 with a 620 'Brownie' B box camera which I'd been given for Christmas and I've just been looking at it to get the description right; it's in its original carrying case containing helpful hints for better pictures and everything is in perfect working order – after over 75 years!

Whenever I get the chance I sneak in a few words about flying boats, because I was so lucky to have that year from 1945 to 46 based in Augusta, Sicily, which was an overnight stopping place on the first stage of BOAC's flying boat service from Poole (later Southampton) to South Africa and the Far East; and I never got tired of watching them taking off or landing. Such a pity that this type of aircraft is no longer in service.

Mahalaow on a visit to Oxford.

Mahalaow relaxes on the beach in the Isle of Wright
during a break while studying for his PhD.

Art and wife, Evy, with son, Brian, on my first visit to Vancouver in 1986.

Evy's 80th birthday party.
Clockwise: Evy, Art, Lori (daughter), Brian (son)
Wil (Lori's husband) and Mary Anne (Brian's wife).

Royal Hudson preserved steam train.

Sunset over Vancouver.

Some of my hobbies.

My Hornby Railway engine which cost £1150.

My home-made sundial
showing the different angles for each hour of sunlight.

CHAPTER 8
More Travels

After that long cruise in the *Canberra* from Hong Kong back to Southampton, I found cruising to be an ideal way for a solo elderly person to be on holiday and began a series of cruises which virtually covered the world. One such memorable trip was on the *QE2* from Southampton to New York and as all the Tourist accommodation was full, I splashed out and went First Class – well worth the extra cost because I elected to sit for dinner each evening at a table for 6 in the Queen's Grill where 3 of my companions were wealthy Arabs from Dubai; one of about 35 with his wife and elder brother who was on his own. They seemed to like me so we got on very well. Their nightly activities always took place in the casino and each morning I'd say, "How did you get on last night?" and the answer would either be, "We lost $50,000" or "We made $200,000" and because they were so wealthy neither result gave them any excitement or worry. How very sad, I used to think. Once I was telling them about my classic Hillman Minx convertible car – then 30 years old. When I asked what they had, there were Bentleys and Rolls Royces as well as less expensive makes in England where they had a London flat and the same sort of thing in Dubai. When we got to New York and said our goodbyes, they gave me an invitation to visit them in Dubai and I could kick myself now for never making the effort to do so.

On another cruise I met a couple who had both been in the forces and based in Gibraltar during the Second World War and had been involved in the story of 'The Man that Never Was' – a high-ranking British officer washed up on a Spanish Mediterranean beach with secret plans on him. They told me how they had to go to well-known places in Spain and do some urgent intentional careless talk to make sure the Germans got to know of these plans, which were of course totally misleading. The possible danger to these plans of deception were that the local Spanish population might decide to bury the body before higher authority had had time to deal with it by the military. The deception was successful.

On a lighter note I was in the bar on our first night at sea on the very new *Oriana* and sitting not far away was an attractive oriental lady wearing a fine silk blouse and an orchid in her hair, and with her (as I soon found out) was her English husband. I picked up my drink and went over to their table with 2 empty chairs and said, "Do you mind if I join you?" and this was the first of our regular meetings for a drink each evening before dinner. The husband had a nursery for producing alstroemerias all the year round for which he held the Royal Warrant from Buckingham Palace to supply fresh cuttings on a daily basis. His wife was from Thailand and after the cruise I was invited to their home which was in Sussex not far from Worthing. The Chelsea Flower Show was not far off and I was asked if I'd help man his stall on one of the days – which I did, arriving at 7.30am and staying on till well into the evening. He gave me a couple of pots of 'alstros' and £100 and when I planted them in the garden of my cottage in Kent, they had spread so rapidly I now had about 10 plants, all flowering vigorously after about 2 or 3 years.

Of all the sea trips that I've made – at least 15 – the one that stands out most is when I visited my Vancouver cousins for the first time in 1986. At that time there was a Polish company which operated a regular service between Poland and Montreal, calling at Tilbury, so I decided to go there and back between Tilbury and Montreal. The ship was called *Stefan Batory*, a later version of the *Stefan Batory* that I was on in 1945 between Malta and Toulon.

I had a huge cabin to Montreal all to myself because the ship was only half full and I was very interested to try their famed beetroot soup which was good. At my table was a former Ship's Pilot from Liverpool with his wife, both now living in Falmouth in order to keep in touch with the sea. He became friendly with the Ship's Chief Engineer so when a special visit was made to the engine room I was invited to go too and I must say I was impressed by that very long revolving metal shaft that was driving the propeller.

After about 7 days from Tilbury we reached the mouth of the St Lawrence River and I mentally felt we were almost there; but we continued for 3 more whole days, sailing up the river until we got to Montreal. After 3 days in Montreal where I had to speak French on a number of occasions, my plans took me to Chicago where I arrived on a Sunday evening with nowhere booked to stay. After one or two enquiries I was recommended to try the Bismarck Hotel, a somewhat older looking building. Yes, they did have a vacancy at $75 but as it was Sunday the price was $45. Although it was quite late, about 9.00pm, the dining room was still open and I had an excellent dinner in very civilised surroundings. My bedroom was also nicely furnished with moulded ceiling and the TV was showing the 'Benny Hill Show'! A quick look round the city after breakfast and the very obvious item of interest was the overhead railway above the streets, which looked strangely antiquated. At 2.30pm I took my place in the train for 2 nights and 3 days to Seattle. During that journey I had all my meals in the dining car which provided the best food throughout my few days in the USA and also at very reasonable prices. At times I rode in the observation coach and at one stage I got talking to a young chap of about 23 or so who was going on holiday to Las Vegas. I asked him where he was going to stay and his surprising reply was, "Nowhere, I stay up all night gambling and find any old place to sleep during the day." What a wasted life I thought. At that age I delighted in going Youth Hostelling in Devon and Cornwall or the wilds of Scotland. Our journey was going to take us through Denver, the Colorado Rockies, and Salt Lake City after which we made a stop at Thompson where one person with a small suitcase got out of the train. There was a wooden hut not far from the railway line and a few trees beyond but nothing else as far as the eye could see in any direction, so where that solitary person was going, I had no idea.

On the third day we reached our destination, Seattle, where I stayed one night and managed to catch up on some of the lost sleep on the train even though my sleeping berth was quite comfortable. American rail tracks do make a bit of noise and cause the coaches to sway quite a lot. We were now quite close to the border and it was only a fairly short coach ride across the border to Vancouver, where I was to stay with my cousins for 3 weeks. We had met 8 years earlier when Art and his wife Evy came to England but now I was going to meet the rest of the family, and I can't say how many cousins. Their son Brian was soon to get married but when I arrived we took a photo and although he was then 26, and I 64, there is obviously a striking similarity in our looks which is not surprising since his father's father and my father were brothers. Art and I soon got on very familiar terms because as I've said earlier we both have the same quirky sense of humour in that we love the sound of funny words.

Brian's job took him into the forests of British Columbia where he supervised the planting of new trees to replace those which had been harvested. I had a memorable experience camping with him when he took me into the mountains above Whistler to spend the night high up near a glacier called the Overlord glacier. There was a full moon and we had spent the night in a tent; just before he dropped off to sleep I said, "What about bears?" and his nonchalant reply was, "Oh, there are a few black ones but they shouldn't bother us." Needless to say, I never slept a wink and lay watching the moonlight on the canvas waiting for the shadow of a paw to appear at any moment to the accompaniment of hooting owls in the forest. Next morning Brian said he wanted to go and look at the glacier but I decided it was too rocky for me, so packed up the tent and waited. One hour went by and I couldn't see any sign of him; then another, by which time I wondered if he'd slipped and couldn't get back. I was on the point of going down the mountain side to raise the alarm but gave another series of loud whistles with my fingers between my teeth and took my white shirt off to wave it about. At last, I saw a small movement in the distance but it was not coming towards me. I went on waving and whistling and after a very anxious hour or so we were re-united. The reason he was not coming to where I was whistling

122

was because its echo was bouncing off the side of the mountain and at first he was heading in the direction of the echo. What a day! One I shall never forget but I'm very glad to have had such an experience.

During the time I spent in Vancouver, Art took me to Vancouver Island where I met several more members of the Priest family. We also went up to Sproat Lake where the 2 huge flying boats known as Water Bombers were based to act as firemen for putting out forest fires. I had earlier written to the manager of the base to ask if we could be taken out to look over one of them and this he had kindly agreed to. When we arrived he introduced us to one of the pilots and we were promptly taken out to one of the aircraft. They were built in 1944 by the Martin Mars company with the idea of carrying nearly 400 military personnel across the Pacific to the Japanese theatre of war, but by the time they were ready for this the war came to a sudden end with the dropping of the 2 atomic bombs.

An aeroplane that could carry between 3 and 400 people was almost unbelievable in 1944 and these flying boats had a wingspan of 202ft, much greater than the jumbo jets which went into general use about 1970. When we climbed inside this monster the pilot then told us how they dealt with putting out fires. They had been specially adapted with a scoop in the centre of the hull and as the flying boat skimmed over the water at just above stalling speed, about 73 mph, the scoop would be gently lowered into the water and within 22 seconds 30 tons of water would fill the inside tank. They would then fly to the scene of the fire, drop the water which had had fire repellent material added to it, go back to the lake and repeat the process; this could go on for 5 hours without a break for refuelling.

This was a very exciting and unusual event for me since my experiences of flying boats in Sicily in 1945 were of much smaller machines that could only carry up to about 30 people.

When it was time for me to leave Vancouver, Art and Evy took me to the railway station to catch the train for the long journey to Montreal. I was a bit disappointed that it left at 4.00pm because I had hoped to do that first part of the journey through the Rockies in daylight. When I settled down in my sleeping berth, it had a large window I could look out of as I lay back on my pillow. By now it was dark and there was a full moon shining in a cloudless sky and as the train wound its way through the mountain passes, the moonlight glistened on the many snow-covered peaks, a truly wonderful sight, more dramatic than in daylight.

We had a prolonged break of journey in Winnipeg when I could leave the train and have a brief look round this forlorn place. I could find nothing in its favour and the long bitterly cold winters must have been very hard to bear. Its main reason for existence was to act as the focal point for the distribution of the huge amounts of grain grown on the prairies. I was very glad when we got on the move again. At Montreal the *Stefan Batory* was tied up waiting to take us back to Tilbury, and the last 2 or 3 days before we arrived were in quite rough seas which didn't put me off my food at all even though the dining room was much emptier than usual. This will probably remain as one of the most memorable journeys of my life – ignoring my RAF days.

I think the most varied cruise I made during this period involved flying to Australia and spending a few days staying with friends in Sydney before joining *Canberra* again for a voyage through the Pacific to Japan. On the way we called at Guam which was the base from which the atomic bomb was flown to be dropped on Hiroshima – a rather chilling experience for the imagination.

When we reached Japan at Kobe I wanted to see the Bullet Train; one of the first High Speed Trains at that time. I walked to the railway station and stood at a spot overlooking the station and I knew what time one of these trains was due. As it came into view, another train – a slow one – came on the adjacent track in the opposite direction completely blocking my view of the fast train. A few months after my visit, Kobe suffered a very serious earthquake and I remember seeing pictures of the elevated motorway under which I had walked, completely in ruins.

Kagoshima was another port of call with pouring rain throughout the day. In spite of this I took a very satisfying photograph of 3 or 4 Japanese people standing on a bridge above a lake, all with different shaped umbrellas. It was a very typical Japanese-style picture with the dim outline of a mountain in the background.

The cruise ended at Singapore where I had made arrangements with a schoolmaster friend to stay at the flat of one of his pupils and his mother. I was there for 9 days and at one point I said I would like to visit a typical South Pacific island. What I had in mind was an exotic sunny beach with silver sand and clear blue sea. When I was taken to Tiomen Island that was exactly what I saw, complete with straw huts right next to the sea where we slept. It took 3 hours to get there across the open sea from Mersing and in those days there wasn't even an airfield there.

It so happened that while I was in Singapore the schoolmaster's daughter was getting married and a 4½-year-old grandson was going to be a page. I was invited to the wedding ceremony and when this little page came down the aisle dressed in velvet with a bow tie, he looked so attractive taking his duties very seriously.

As a tourist attraction, a replica of an ancient village had been built at one end of Singapore Island and many shops and activities had been created there to show what life was like in the distant past.

One of the peculiarities of life in Singapore is that you need to take something warm to put on when you go shopping because the air conditioning is set much too high and as soon as you enter the places that have it, the contrast is so great you need to put on something extra.

My 9 days ended with a visit to the parents of one of my earliest student visitors. When I got to know him he asked me if I knew of somewhere in London for his sister and parents to stay. I had plenty of space for all 4 of them in my house so I said they could stay with me. The sister was a stewardess with Singapore Airlines so mum and dad could get here for nothing. While they were staying with me, I made some currant buns and the sister was watching how I did this. When the fat was added to the mixture she said, "Is that lard?" I knew immediately what she was getting at so quickly said, "No, it's a form of margarine" – which put her mind at ease. When the family had tea that day the mother commented how nice the buns were!

Back in Singapore the day came when I went to the airport for the flight home and as I said goodbye to my friends, I was given an enormous plastic box full of orchids and when the stewardess saw me struggling with it she said, "Give it to me and I'll put it in the cold area," which saved me a lot of trouble.

These cruises on *Canberra* in the Far East had been so successful I decided to join her in Sydney once more. I discovered that many people had a strong feeling of affection for the ship as I did and each time I went aboard her I would meet quite a number of people that I'd met on previous voyages. I think this feeling originated from the fact that *Canberra* had done her bit during the Falklands War of 1982 when she was then, in nautical terms, getting on in years and some referred to her as 'The Old Lady'.

My destination this time was to be Bombay where I would leave the ship and travel to New Delhi. I did some careful planning for the 9 days that I would be in India on my own and not on any package tour, so got a book out of the library called *India by Rail*. This was such a blessing because one of the most important pieces of advice was to plan all train journeys well in advance before leaving home then go to the All India Railways Office near Wembley Stadium to buy every railway ticket I should be needing in advance, at that office. I'd planned to go from Bombay to Delhi; Delhi to Shimla via Kalka; Delhi to Jaipur and Delhi to Agra – all First Class.

After a quick look round Bombay when I left the ship, I got the 5.00pm train for the 16-hour overnight journey to Delhi and on entering the station the ticket office was besieged by a crowd which looked as though they were trying to get to see a football match. Fortunately my ticket had the number of the coach and seat on it and this was pasted on a board beside the entrance door to the carriage. I found this surprisingly efficient considering those numbers had been allocated to me in Wembley. Inside the coach I had a berth in a 4-berth sleeper and my companions were a very smart Indian with his 2 sons of about 10 to 12, all speaking perfect English. The train was packed solid except for the First Class areas which we occupied and 2 hours after the journey started we were served with a very good meal on a tray, similar to aircraft meals. I had a very pleasant conversation with these three until we decided to get ready for sleep with sheets and pillows. I slept surprisingly well, waking up to a good breakfast, and dead on 9.00am we arrived on schedule in New Delhi.

Before leaving home I had contacted the BBC's correspondent in India, Mark Tully, to ask if I could leave my main suitcase in his office, so outside the station I took one of these 3-wheel tuk-tuks to his address. On the way, whenever we stopped for traffic, little beggar children would rush up and ask for money but what I found most disturbing, little girls of 5 or 6 would brush the dust off my shoes with their long hair.

Having got rid of the heavy bag, I was now free to find my way to the YMCA where I had booked a very comfortable room. They served a lot of English-style meals especially at breakfast time, as well as local dishes.

One morning I asked to be woken at 4.00am as I was going to Jaipur on the 5.00am train. When they knocked at my door they had a tray of breakfast for me which I never expected. The journey took 5 hours and I returned on the same day, getting in by 11.00pm, both train journeys running on time.

When I went to Shimla I had read in that library book that one of the drivers on the train from Kalka to Shimla was called R. Singh Gill who was also an artist who had exhibitions of his paintings in various parts of India. As I was waiting on the platform at Kalka to join this train, a big man wearing a turban came striding up to me and said, "Do you know who I am?" I thought to myself, why should I? But I suppose it may have been because I was the only white person in sight, so I said (remembering the passage in the book), "You're not Mr R. Singh

Gill are you?" to which his face lit up and he said, "Yes!" Because of that he invited me to ride in the driver's cabin with him on the 93km, 5-hour journey climbing 7,000ft to Shimla.

In the course of this journey we discussed his art work and he invited me to his house where many of his pictures were hung round the walls. It then became obvious why he'd made the invitation because when we got there he said, "Have a good look round and tell me which one you'd like to buy." There was one which I quite liked showing a pine forest and distant view of the Himalayas. When I chose it he said, "Most people pay me £100," but I eventually got it for £40 and he said, "I'll collect the rest next time I come to London."

On the way up in the train he asked me why I was travelling to Shimla and the main reason was that I wanted to see the building where previous viceroys had spent the summer months to escape the heat down in the plains. It had been designed by a Scotsman, Henry Irwin, and opened in 1888. Lord Mountbatten was the last person to occupy it in his official vice-regal capacity. Mr Gill said he knew the man who now ran it as a conference centre and place of learning so he would take me there in the morning. He then said I could stay the night in his house. I was beginning to feel very cold and there had even been a snow shower so at bedtime there was a mattress on the floor and he filled a hot water bottle and gave it to me. I kept all my clothes on all night and before dropping off to sleep, he got on to the other side of the mattress, still wearing his turban and said, "Now it's my turn to have the hot water bottle."

Next morning he took me to the Viceregal Lodge and introduced me to a very learned and cultured Indian. Mr Gill left us to drive the train back to Kalka and I was given a wonderful private tour of the whole building. The 2 rooms that impressed me most were Lord Louis's private bathroom with huge mirrors on every wall and a spectacular view of the Himalaya range, then the Banqueting Hall where imprints were still visible on the panelled walls where rifles had once hung in different patterns.

In the course of this tour I was told how Lady Mountbatten had heard Lord Louis and Pandit Nehru raising their voices to one another over plans for the partition of India and when things showed signs of getting overheated she burst in and told them both to stop squabbling like a couple of naughty children and get down to some serious business.

After such an interesting morning I was intrigued by the number of monkeys that were everywhere jumping about in the trees as I walked back to the centre of the town. Because I had not realised how cold it was going to be I kept my pyjamas on under my light summer clothes but that wasn't much better so I cut short my visit and returned to the lower levels. On the way down I rode in one of the carriages this time and was able to appreciate the wonderful views as the train wound its way round spiral tunnels in order to lose height more quickly. It was a narrow gauge track railway and the coaches were quite short. When we stopped at various areas it amused me to see a sign over the doorway to a small booking office type place which said 'Assistant Deputy Director' – of what, I could not imagine.

It was a welcome change to get back to the warm areas again and my next trip took me to see the Taj Mahal at Agra, a much shorter journey this time from Delhi. On the train I got talking to a very smart Indian who turned out to be a famous surgeon. He told me he had recently seen a British MP who had travelled to India specially for treatment by him.

On arrival at the Taj Mahal I was surprised to find how much bigger it was than I expected as I stood under the dome. I suppose it was because the majority of photos are taken from some way off in order to get the whole building in the picture. I managed to get an unusual shot of several Japanese monks in their colourful robes all walking down one side of the paved area holding fans over their heads to keep the sun out of their eyes.

On my return to the station to get the train back to Delhi we were told there was an unavoidable delay due to a tiger further up the line on the track. During that delay a 17-year-old boy wanted to talk to me about life in Britain. He was very well educated so I guess he was wondering how he might find a job in the UK.

One of the last things I did before returning home was join a tour of the city by coach and at a certain quiet spot by the roadside we stopped and gathered round 2 men who were going to show us a trick. One of them lay down on a sandy area with 2 long poles, one either side of him parallel to his body. His partner then proceeded to cover him and the poles completely with a large heavy looking tarpaulin sheet. The partner then started to beat a small drum very rapidly and the 2 poles began to rise from the ground under the sheet, which was draped over them. All that was visible of the man underneath it was his head sticking out of one end while his feet were still covered but you could see where they were. The sheet rose higher and higher until it was at least 3 or 4 feet clear of the ground and you could see daylight in all directions underneath it. There it stayed for a short while with the man's head still visible and feet sticking up underneath and then slowly it descended to its original position on the ground. The man jumped up from it leaving the 2 poles on the ground under the sheet and proceeded to bring his hat round to us all for his reward. It was really dramatic and the only thing I noticed was that one of his thumbs had a small gash which was bleeding slightly.

Throughout my 9 days alone in India I never felt any sense of fear or apprehension, even walking through the market area of Shimla after dark. At Jaipur I had been fascinated by the huge sundial constructed, I think, 200 or more years ago by one of the Maharajas. The gnomon of this sundial was as tall as a 2-storey building and cast a shadow that could measure the time by the sun to an accuracy of 3 seconds.

After such a varied and interesting holiday as this had been, it was difficult to imagine any other that might be compared with it, yet 3 years later I did have a wonderful 3 weeks in Vietnam.

For some years I had known a Vietnamese family who came to this country as refugees. For a short time the husband had worked in the BBC Vietnamese Service at Bush House and when his sister died he was able to return to Vietnam for her funeral. While he was there he sent me a telegram saying he could be my guide if I liked to join him in Saigon (now Ho Chi Minh City). When I got there he said a cousin of his had lent him his car complete with driver for the whole 3-week period. The driver's name was Yap, in his early 30s and with quite good English.

We set out to drive north up the coast to Nha Trang. The hotel had special quarters for anyone that could be described as 'staff', so Yap had his own room in a different part of the hotel. My friend had relatives in this area and they were so surprised to see him when we called on them because not long before, they had heard his voice over the radio in the Vietnamese Service. Calling on members of his family like this made a big difference from the usual kind of overseas visits because we were visiting local inhabitants and seeing what their everyday lives were like.

I was quite surprised to see very little evidence of the dreadful years of war that had not long finished. We were told that a magnificent golf course was under construction which was eventually going to be suitable for World Open Championship events. When we visited Dalat, situated in the hills north of Saigon, there was a distinct French influence to the place with broad tree-lined avenues containing very elegant French-looking houses. Dalat was a favourite place for wealthy people to spend the summer months when the weather was very hot at lower levels. I found the local food so much to my liking because their main source of flavouring was many different herbs all with a tendency to lemon flavour and no hot chillies or overpowering garlic. At one village where we stopped for lunch in a very simple café, I had one of the best chicken meals of the lot and was happily eating it with chopsticks. This intrigued the locals because they'd hardly seen any Westerners and one who was using chopsticks brought a small crowd round my table to watch me using them.

The Vietnamese were charming in every way and when we were invited to a wedding banquet, I found myself sitting next to one of the relatives. She was a fairly large lady in her late 40s I should think and although we couldn't exchange a single word with each other she fussed over me and pointed out the best things to eat, like a hen looking after its chicks. I thoroughly enjoyed her company.

When the bride and groom arrived at the steps of the banqueting hall, we were already seated at our various tables and the first we knew of their arrival was a huge salvo of Chinese cracker fireworks – one of their traditions I was told.

The last trip we made in the borrowed car was to a seaside resort not far from Saigon called Vung Tau and sitting on the beach, drying off after a dip in the sea was hardly any different from doing the same thing at home. This was because it was September and the weather was just right and not too hot. When we drove back to hand over the car and its driver who had done all the navigating for us, I hope we gave him a good present because if we did, I can't remember what it was. I expect it was money because that would have been most useful to him. When I got back to England I almost immediately went to my favourite spot in Cornwall for a week's walking round the coastal footpaths both sides of Land's End, always a spectacular land and seascape.

Some time after that when I got back from Vietnam, Evy and Art, my cousins in Vancouver, planned to celebrate their Ruby Wedding Anniversary. Because it's not one of the major celebration dates they didn't expect me to attend. It so happened that Johnny and Mary, my cousins in England, were about to go on their first cruise, and this was going to Alaska, starting from Vancouver. By coincidence they would be able to go to the "Ruby Do", as Mary called it, before sailing. In these circumstances I felt I would secretly go to Vancouver without telling Evy or Art and surprise them by turning up in the middle of their celebrations. I arranged with their daughter Lori and husband Wil that I would stay with them for a couple of nights before the great day; then when they were having the party in Evy and Art's garden, Lori and her brother Brian would announce a surprise and I would walk up the garden path from the gate at the bottom of the garden. It all worked perfectly except while I was hiding outside the garden gate. Mary's husband Johnny was standing in a spot overlooking the place where I was waiting and I dodged out of sight just in time before he turned to look in that direction, so my surprise appearance did work very well. Their cruise was a great success much to Johnny's surprise because I'd been trying to persuade him for a long time that he would enjoy such a holiday. He always maintained that after many years flying as a captain for BOAC all over the world, he would be bored stiff. After this trip he had to admit he'd enjoyed it and went on several more cruises after this one.

Having made quite a few trips to the Far East, I now turned my attention to the Norwegian Fjords and it had recently been announced that *Canberra* was due to be withdrawn from service in a year's time. Before that she was due to go on such a trip to Norway, so for the 5th and last time I booked to go on her to the Land of the Midnight Sun. It was wonderful and we even called at the most northerly Post Office in the world at Spitsbergen. While anchored off-shore for our postcards to be posted, I saw a huge chunk of glacier break off and fall into the sea. It was 2.00am and the sun was shining so the captain announced he was going to take us further north to the edge of the permanent pack-ice, but on the way we could see a bank of fog and reluctantly we had to turn round and retrace our route. The captain did say that at that point when we turned round we'd been above 80° latitude, further north than *Canberra* had ever been before.

The following year when the ship was retired I heard that it was going to sail to Karachi to be broken up but her final captain whilst in service refused to take her on such an emotional journey. *Canberra* had been built in the days when there had been a regular service by sea between the UK and Australia and this had been her early role for several years until the service was terminated and she was converted into a cruise ship which had such an appeal to many regular passengers. This was in spite of shortcomings such as cabins with no en suite facilities. I once shared a 2-berth cabin with a gentleman and it was so small we had to wait for each other to dress because there was not enough room for both of us to use the cabin at the same time. I stayed in the top bunk out of the way when it was my turn to wait. On one of the days when the ship was rolling a bit in the rough sea, I had hung my sponge bag on the rail underneath the wash basin and during the morning when the cabin was empty the bag had slipped off the rail and unfortunately straight into the waste-paper basket which was below it. The cabin steward had been in to tidy up and of course empty the basket and I lost all my bathroom equipment.

Because of the shortage of en suite facilities there were large rooms with about 12 washbasins in a row on one side and toilets on the other but very few bathrooms in a different part of the corridor. These areas were always spotlessly clean and the cleaner of the one I used most was from Goa. He always had a cheery word with me and at the end of the cruise I gave him a tip. About 2 years later when I was making my first voyage on the new *Oriana*, I had been shown to my cabin and on the dressing table was a card saying I would be sitting in the dining room at table 106. As it was only 5.00pm and the place was empty I went to see just where number 106 was situated and as I did so a waiter came in wearing a very smart colourful waist coat. As he saw me he came over and said, "Hello Mr Priest; nice to see you again." I was so surprised to hear him call me by my name and I said, "How did you know my name?" to which he replied, "We met on the *Canberra* 2 years ago." What a wonderful memory, considering all the masses of people he'd encountered in the meantime because he was now in a much better position as a wine waiter.

At this stage of affairs I was now pretty familiar with large areas of the Far East and North America as well as the Mediterranean, so choosing my next cruise gave me something to think about until I happened to see a piece about Voyages of Discovery. The one that appealed to me started from Harwich and went via the Faroes, Iceland and Greenland ending up at St. John's in Newfoundland then flying home. This sounded too good to miss so I decided to go on it in August 2005. The biggest surprise of this venture was to discover how fascinating and unexpectedly interesting everything was throughout the voyage, particularly Greenland. The duration of the cruise was 17 days and as soon as

I was on board I met the five other people I was to share a table with for dinner each evening – always a gamble but this time first impressions were very good. Similarly I was very pleased to have a decent cabin to myself.

Our first port of call was Torshavn (pronounced Torshown to rhyme with 'gown') – the main town in the Faroe Islands, always mentioned in the BBC shipping forecast. This was a much bigger place than I had imagined and was surrounded by large areas of lush green grass. I believe keen fishermen go there a lot on holiday. When we got to Reykjavik, the capital of Iceland, our tour took us to the Blue Lagoon where many people were bathing in very blue and very warm water – so warm in fact that parts of it are fenced off because to go beyond the fence the water would be much too hot for comfort. One is constantly reminded of the volcanic nature of Iceland in general. I believe the whole of Reykjavik is centrally heated by the natural high temperature of parts of the ground just below the surface. There is also a spot where you can see how the earth fault between East and West is actually getting wider by measurable amounts each year. I decided to walk through the streets of the town back to the ship and on the way I passed through a residential area and a whole family were sunbathing on the lawn in front of their house so I thought what an unusual photo it would make of a group of people sunbathing in Iceland. I stopped by their gate and said, "Excuse me, would you mind if I took your photo, sunbathing in Iceland?" They all came over to me and spoke in perfect English and I explained why I thought it would make an unusual photo. They all agreed and re-arranged themselves for which I thanked them all very much and we parted happily. An hour later when I was back on the ship I could have kicked myself for not taking a note of their address so that I could have sent them a copy of the photo.

Our next port of call was to be Greenland but on the way there the captain came on the tannoy and said that in view of the perfect weather conditions he was going to take us through the 55-mile channel of Prins Christian Sund at the southern tip of Greenland. We travelled very slowly northwards with great mountains either

135

side, rather like the Norwegian Fjords except our channel was open both ends.

As we progressed we gradually overtook a small motor boat with only one man in it. When we got closer we could see he was towing 2 dead seals and you could clearly see the gashes where he'd had to kill them. We then became aware of children's voices cheering and waving to us from a small plateau at the foot of a huge mountain. There were 5 of them, all under about 12 or 14, and the motor boat was bringing them vital supplies. We were told that a supply ship can only visit them twice a year because weather conditions make it too difficult during the depths of winter. Their plateau just above the water level was the only place where they could live because everywhere else the steep mountains went down straight into the sea, and to go anywhere had to be by boat.

Our ship must have been a very rare sight for the little ones waving to us and as we passed by, really quite close to them. I became very emotional to think of their lonely and isolated existence. This strange eerie feeling, difficult to put into words, intensified as the sound of their young voices drifted over the still waters and faded away into nothing, leaving a silence I shall never forget.

Next day presented another surprise when we anchored at Narsarsuak made famous by the Viking Erik the Red who settled here in AD 985. What made it so memorable for me was the fact that as we tramped along a grassy track there was a large green field full of sheep contentedly grazing and in the distance I could hear someone playing the organ in a small church. I could easily have been in a part of Sussex near the South Downs. In fact Erik is credited with describing the area as a "very Green-Land".

More surprises came with the next port of call. This time it was Nuuk, the capital of Greenland, and here I was amazed to find blocks of flats, a busy street with traffic lights, a cargo terminal for container ships and even a Chinese takeaway! Fortunately we'd had a lot of good weather which did mean we were seeing these places under ideal conditions, and so when we got to Disco Bay to transfer into smaller motor boats we were able to drift almost noiselessly right up close to the huge floating icebergs as big as Beachy Head. When the engine was switched off, all that could be heard above the deafening silence was the trickle of water as the tops of the icebergs melted in the brilliant sunshine.

So that was Greenland and how lucky I was to have seen it under such favourable conditions. We were now about to enter Canadian waters and the last stage of this truly remarkable cruise.

After a couple of stops on the way south off the coast of Labrador, we arrived at Newfoundland's capital, St John's, made famous by Marconi's first transatlantic radio message – the letter 'S' in Morse Code – having been received there in December 1901 from Cornwall. Charles Lindbergh also took off from there on his 36-hour non-stop flight to Paris in 1927. We took off in much more comfortable conditions on our non-stop flight to Gatwick.

I was so pleased to have made this true Voyage of Discovery because it had been just that and so full of surprises.

Day-to-day life at home was often occupied in trying to find spare parts for my Hillman Minx convertible which was now quite firmly in the category of a Classic Car, being well over 40 years old. I often got a friendly toot on the horn of a passing car of similar vintage and the outward appearance was still very smart – having had a new hood only a few years previously. The search for spares was becoming increasingly difficult and very reluctantly I decided to buy a new Hyundai car for everyday use and keep the Hillman for special occasions. This arrangement didn't last long though because cars of any age don't like standing in a garage for any length of time without being used. After several unsuccessful attempts to find a buyer, the day finally arrived when I drove the car out of its garage for the last time and took it to Worthing where my cousin took a photo of me in the driving seat on the way to the new owner.

I'd had the car for 44 years and driven over 150,000 miles in it with complete safety and only a handful of breakdowns – and these invariably happened when it was quite convenient to put things right. I always enjoyed driving it and hated parting with it so now all I have is that last photo in a frame on my lounge mantelpiece.

The regular almost weekly visits to my cottage in Kent were abruptly terminated on 10th May 2011 when I woke up to discover I could hardly see out of my left eye and on arrival at the Emergency Department at the local eye hospital it was discovered that a vein had burst at the back of the eye. Driving was out of the question because I had been under treatment for several years for both eyes which had Glaucoma and the right eye alone was not good enough to carry on driving.

When you own a second property it's lovely to be able to go there whenever you like, particularly if it's only just over half an hour away by car. The trouble is that no matter which place you are in at any one time, you have the nagging worry of wondering if everything is alright in the other. This especially applies during bad weather conditions – e.g. I wonder if the pipes have frozen or did that gale damage the roof? Without a car it would take me at least two and a half hours to get to the cottage by public transport and without my own car it would be difficult to take goods and materials for each visit.

So the major decision was soon made that I would have to sell my cottage in Kent which had given me so much pleasure for exactly 30 years. It went on the market in August 2011 and the sale took place just 4 months later. I was very pleased that a delightful family with young children became the new owners and as they had been attracted by the way I had intentionally made the interior look old-fashioned with good quality second-hand items, they very willingly agreed to buy the place exactly as it stood complete with furniture and fittings and my beautiful Ritmüller Boudoir Grand piano.

This left a big hole in my life all within the space of 6 months – no more weekends away from Carshalton and no more driving cars. It took some getting used to especially as reading books and looking at television was no longer at all easy.

Fortunately I was still able to get about on my own and I soon created the habit of going to lunch-time concerts at St James's

Church in Piccadilly which take place on Mondays, Wednesdays and Fridays throughout every month. I prefer piano recitals but occasionally find guitar solos or piano and strings can be very interesting. One thing I always avoid is sopranos – in fact almost any kind of singing; unless the singer is bang on the note it grates like a knife scraping a plate with me.

After each visit I go to the adjoining Caffé Nero for a sandwich late lunch and half an hour in the upstairs armchairs, and very often go on to a museum with a particular display or the Royal Academy which is almost opposite the church. In this way I am able to spend a leisurely day out in London by leaving home around 11.00am and returning in time for a cup of tea at about 5.00pm. Living less than 200 yards from the Network Rail local station and with frequent double-decker red buses passing my house I couldn't wish for a better public transport system all covered by the Freedom Pass which I use almost every day of the week, so much so that I know the bus and train timetables almost by heart, except during rush hours when I try to avoid travelling. It's also worth trying to avoid getting on buses after lunch when the school children are coming out of school.

On the subject of going to school by train or bus it's an interesting fact that during the 5 years from the age of 12 to 17 when I used the train every day to and from school, not once was I ever late due to trains not being on time, whereas today the situation is not nearly so reliable.

During the 3 years between 1936 and 1939 at Epsom College, we used Epsom Downs station which is still the terminus of that particular line. In those early years it had one day of glory each year – Derby Day, and all the many platforms came into use to accommodate the special luxury Pullman steam trains which came from all over England. The line from Sutton to Epsom Downs is a 4-mile gruelling uphill climb for these heavy trains and an extra engine had to push the back of the train to help the main engine at the front up the severe gradient. Even so our trains to and from school got through on time, although once in school we weren't allowed outside the grounds until it was time to go home.

Some years later when I was a cashier in Lloyds Bank, Banstead, which is very near Epsom Race Course, we had a rather similar arrangement because in 1949 and 1950 Derby Day was always on a Wednesday and Head Office decided that we should close at twelve noon on those days. On one of those days I cycled over to the race course and put 2 shillings (10p) on a horse and won 6 shillings, 30p in today's money, and I was lucky not to lose my bike in the process.

As I recall more and more of my impressions which have mostly been in chronological order, I seem to have slipped back in time with these last few thoughts, never more so than when I still get a Christmas card from the widow of the builder who made such a wonderful job of converting the 2 adjoining cottages, which my aunt left me, into one most attractive cottage. By a strange coincidence his builder's yard was situated right next to the Bessels Green house where I was born, which very neatly completes the circle – and circles have no end, nor does my story.

The unusual overhead railway above a Chicago street.

Art shows me round Vancouver Harbour
and takes me to see the Water Bombers (overleaf).

141

My private conducted tour of the Water Bombers took place
on Sproat Lake, Vancouver Island.

Drifting among icebergs in Disco Bay, Greenland.

Huge icebergs in Disco Bay.

2am in Arctic waters.

St. John's Newfoundland – made famous by
Marconi's first trans-Atlantic radio signal.

Photo taken by a member of a special tour I was taking round the Croydon Airport Museum on 25th November 2012.

Airport House, the first purpose-built airport terminal building in the world, opened in 1928. This photo was taken about 25 years after Croydon Airport finally closed in 1959 and the building is now the entrance to the Croydon Airport Museum.

Six snapshots taken at Croydon Airport by me
during a guided tour of the apron and hangars in 1939.

The Beeches Avenue where I live, on the left.
Just over half mile further on are Carshalton Ponds.

Part of the River Wandle flows through the Carshalton Ponds,
and the parish church is where my father and his brother, Albert, sang
in the choir.